Python For Beginners

A Practical and Step-by-Step Guide to Programming with Python

Daniel Correa – Paola Vallejo

Practical Books

Copyright © 2023 by Daniel Correa and Paola Vallejo
All rights reserved.

Python For Beginners

by Daniel Correa and Paola Vallejo
Copyright © 2023 by Daniel Correa and Paola Vallejo.

All rights are reserved. No part of this book may be reproduced, stored in any system, or transmitted in any form or by any means without prior authorization from the authors, except for brief citations for articles or reviews.

Great effort has been made to prepare this book and to ensure the information's accuracy. However, the information contained in this book is sold without warranty, either express or implied. Neither the author nor its distributors shall be liable for any damages caused or allegedly caused directly or indirectly by this book.

Technical Editors: Ronald M. Martinod and Simón E. Suárez.

Code Reviewers: Juliana Parra and Juan Felipe Pinzón.

First edition: May 2023.

To my incredible wife Juliana, your support has been crucial in this journey.
- Daniel Correa

To my family for their unconditional support.
- Paola Vallejo

Contributors

About the authors

Daniel Correa is a professor, researcher, software developer, and author of multiple programming books. He has a Ph.D. in Computer Science and is a professor at Universidad EAFIT in Medellin, Colombia. He has been a teacher for over ten years and coordinates programming courses. He is interested in software architectures, frameworks (such as Laravel, Nest, Django, Express, Vue, React, and Angular), web development, and clean code. Follow Daniel on Twitter at **@danielgarax**.

Paola Vallejo is a teacher and researcher. She has a Ph.D. in Computer Science. She currently works at Universidad EAFIT in Medellin, Colombia, where she teaches basic programming and software engineering courses. She has been a teacher for more than seven years. She is interested in topics related to software architectures, software design, and clean code.

About the technical editors

Ronald M. Martinod has been an associate professor at Universidad EAFIT since 2015. He completed his education in mechanical engineering and later obtained a Ph.D. from the University of Lorraine (France) in the School of Computer Science and Mathematics Engineering. He gained experience working on research projects that support organizations in optimizing maintenance policies and the operation of urban transport networks.

Simón E. Suárez is an engineering physicist and graduate student from the Applied Physics Master at Universidad EAFIT, Colombia. Some of his current scientific interests are scientific instrumentation, materials science, applications of magnetic nanoparticles, amateur rocketry, plasma physics. He enjoys hands-on experimentation and working in the lab. You can find his LinkedIn profile at https://www.linkedin.com/in/simon-suarez-19106b185/.

About the code reviewers

Juliana Parra is a technical document management administrator. She is passionate about reading and traveling.

Juan Felipe Pinzón is an enthusiastic student pursuing System Engineering at Universidad EAFIT. He is passionate about learning and committed to growing as a well-rounded individual. For more information, visit his LinkedIn profile at https://linkedin.com/in/juan-felipe-pinzón-trejo-319711247.

Table of contents

Preface 7
Chapter 01 – Introduction 11
Chapter 02 – Computers and programming 17
Chapter 03 – Python..25
Chapter 04 – Hello world in Colab..29
Chapter 05 – Int, float, and str variables 41
Chapter 06 – Data input and output 53
Chapter 07 – Simple conditionals...63
Chapter 08 – Multiple conditionals..77
Chapter 09 – While loop...91
Chapter 10 – Strings 105
Chapter 11 – Lists 119
Chapter 12 – Dictionaries 133
Chapter 13 – For loop..147
Chapter 14 – Functions...157
Chapter 15 – Counters, accumulators, and flags 175
Chapter 16 – Files 183
Chapter 17 – Libraries – Matplotlib...195
Chapter 18 – Continue your learning 203
Chapter 19 – Exercise solutions 207

Preface

Programming is everywhere. Having programming skills is essential for this modern world, almost as important as knowing how to write or speak English. Nowadays, "coding" or "programming" has become the language of "innovation".

Programmers have become the rock stars of our time. We recognize individuals like Mark Zuckerberg, Bill Gates, and Elon Musk. And it's no secret that today it is one of the highest-paid professions worldwide.

In this book, we will discover some of the basic mysteries of programming, explain some of the fundamental structures, and develop hundreds of pieces of code.

The big difference between this book and other similar ones is that we will adopt a strategy governed by three fundamental elements: (i) we will develop concepts with a **theoretical/practical** approach, (ii) we will explain each element **step by step**, and (iii) we will use **images** to explain the fundamental elements.

Theoretical/practical: We will explain each concept we develop calmly and briefly, with words that any reader can understand (without going around in circles or using complex expressions). In addition, we will develop multiple pieces of code, examples, and exercises for the reader to practice and understand how to apply each element seen.

Step by step: We will start with short and simple pieces of code. In addition, we will adequately explain each instruction developed. We will not assume that the reader magically understands everything.

Images: We will use supporting images to facilitate the understanding of multiple concepts and pieces of code (both simple and complex). We will use diagrams, step-by-step code flows, and screen outputs for the reader to verify their progress.

Who is this book for?

This book is designed for anyone who wants to learn programming, whether they are young, adults, professionals, or teachers. In addition, it is a book designed for beginners or novices.

The book does not require any prior programming knowledge from the reader. We only recommend that the reader knows how to read, has basic arithmetic knowledge (such as adding and subtracting), can use a computer, and can follow instructions. We will not take anything for granted; if necessary, we will explain everything in this book.

What does this book cover?

As the title indicates, this is a book for beginners. This book covers fundamental programming elements in Python, including topics such as computers, programming, algorithms, variables, conditionals, loops, functions, lists, dictionaries, files, and a brief introduction to libraries. It is a short book designed not to overwhelm the reader. Although it could have covered more topics, only the aforementioned topics are treated to explain them well and in detail.

By the end of the book, the reader will have acquired knowledge of basic elements in programming, which they can then apply in more advanced projects, allowing them to gain new knowledge more easily.

What previous experience do the authors have?

Daniel and Paola have more than 18 years of combined experience in teaching programming. They have also been authors of other web programming books. During these years, they have taught programming to thousands of students from different universities.

In this book, they compile and present many of the strategies used to teach programming to different audiences of students.

General comments

If you have any questions about any aspect of this book, please email us at practicalbooksco@gmail.com and mention the book title in the subject line of your message. Additionally, **we have two extra digital chapters not included with the book, but we will give them as a gift to any reader who writes to us and requests them**.

Errors in the book (errata)

Although multiple people have reviewed the book, and we have taken all precautions to ensure its quality, errors happen. Therefore, if you find any errors in this book, we ask and appreciate that you please write to us at practicalbooksco@gmail.com informing us of the error to be corrected.

Piracy

If you find any illegal link or copy of the book on the Internet or anywhere else, we kindly ask and appreciate that you please provide us with that link or information at practicalbooksco@gmail.com.

Getting a PDF format with colored images

If you purchased the Kindle or print version of this book from Amazon, please email us at practicalbooksco@gmail.com with a screenshot of your Amazon purchase, and we will give you a PDF version that includes all the colored images as a gift.

Getting book updates

If you wish to receive updates on this book, please email us at practicalbooksco@gmail.com, and we will add you to our mailing list.

Chapter 01 – Introduction

We will begin our journey to learn to program with Python. In this book, we will cover many of the essential elements required for computer programming, as well as the main elements of Python.

To get started, in this chapter, we will explain the book's design and how to use it effectively.

Next, we will cover the following sections:
1. Book chapters.
2. How to read this book.
3. Book repository.
4. Cheat sheet.

1.1. Book chapters

This book is divided into 19 chapters. Here's a brief overview of what you can expect to learn in each chapter:
- **Chapter 01 – Introduction.** Provides an overview of the book and its contents.
- **Chapter 02 – Computers and programming.** Introduces the key concepts of computers, programming, programming languages, and algorithms. It also breaks some common myths about programming.
- **Chapter 03 – Python.** Introduces the Python programming language, explains how it compares to other languages, and describes some applications that could be developed using Python.
- **Chapter 04 – Hello world in Colab.** Describes how to use Colab, a popular tool for coding in Python.
- **Chapter 05 – Int, float, and str variables.** Introduces the fundamental concept of variables and covers three types of variables: int, float, and str. It also explains how to display information on the computer screen.
- **Chapter 06 – Data input and output.** Describes how to perform data input and output operations, focusing on the print function (for displaying information) and the input function (for capturing information from the keyboard).
- **Chapter 07 – Simple conditionals.** Introduces basic concepts for handling conditions in programming and shows how to implement a simple conditional based on the *if-then* statement in Python.
- **Chapter 08 – Multiple conditionals.** Develops other conditional statements such as *if-then-else*, *if-then-elif-else*, and nested conditionals to handle multiple conditions in a program.

- **Chapter 09 – While loop.** Introduces the concept of loops in programming and shows how to define and use a while loop.
- **Chapter 10 – Strings.** Explains the importance of string manipulation in programming, presents the properties of strings, and covers some fundamental operations and methods.
- **Chapter 11 – Lists.** Develops the concept of lists and performs basic operations with lists.
- **Chapter 12 – Dictionaries.** Develops the concept of dictionaries and performs basic operations with dictionaries.
- **Chapter 13 – For loop.** Introduces the for loop, another type of loop in Python that allows you to iterate over different types of variables.
- **Chapter 14 – Functions.** Details the behavior of functions in Python and shows how to create functions with multiple variations.
- **Chapter 15 – Counters, accumulators, and flags.** Describes three common programming operations: counting, accumulating, and performing checks over specific conditions.
- **Chapter 16 – Files.** Provides an overview of how to read, write, and analyze file data in Python.
- **Chapter 17 – Libraries – Matplotlib.** Introduces the concept of libraries in Python and demonstrates how to use Matplotlib to create visualizations in Python.
- **Chapter 18 – Continue your learning.** Provides additional resources to continue your learning journey with Python and programming.
- **Chapter 19 – Exercise solutions.** Contains the answer to the exercises proposed throughout the book.

1.2. How to read this book

To make the most out of this book and improve your understanding of the concepts presented, we recommend following these suggestions:

Read in order

If this is your first-time programming, we recommend reading this book in order. The book is designed to learn different concepts and elements in order. These concepts and elements will be reused in later chapters, which means that, for example, to understand and enjoy "Chapter 13 - For loop", you will need to understand almost all previous chapters. For instance, within this chapter, we use various elements such as lists, dictionaries, variables, and strings introduced in previous chapters.

Learning by doing

One of the key elements of this book is "Learning by doing," inspired by one of Daniel and Paola's favorite book authors, Greg Lim. **In this book, you will learn to program by programming**. We have included over 100 independent pieces of code for you to develop, and we strongly recommend that you code them manually. By doing so, you will acquire programming skills and better understand each element used. Take the time to read each piece of code, analyze it in detail, and execute it. This approach will help you master the concepts covered in the book.

TIP: Learning by doing: "Human beings are insatiable seekers of knowledge; however, they do not learn what they hear, read, memorize or study... they learn what they practice." (Taken from: *2019 - Samsó, R. - The Power of Discipline: The Habit that will Change your Life*).

Exercises for practice

At the end of most chapters, you will find a set of simple exercises designed to help you reinforce the concepts and skills learned in that chapter. We strongly recommend completing these exercises before moving on to the next chapter. Doing so will allow you to test your understanding and ensure you have acquired the expected skills. In addition, you will find the solutions to all the exercises in the book's last chapter.

1.3. Book repository

In most chapters, we will write pieces of code in Python. All code pieces developed in this book can be found in the book repository at the following link: https://github.com/PracticalBooks/Python-For-Beginners. If we modify the code later, those modifications will be reflected in the repository.

Questions

If you have any questions or would like to discuss any aspect of this book, we recommend using the discussion area of the book repository, located at https://github.com/PracticalBooks/Python-For-Beginners/discussions (see Figure 1-1). This platform allows you to learn from the questions and discussions posted by other readers, while also enabling you to seek help and interact with the book's authors and community. With the input and contributions from various members, the discussion area can provide a collaborative and enriched learning experience. Please note that to access the "New discussion" button, you will need a GitHub account.

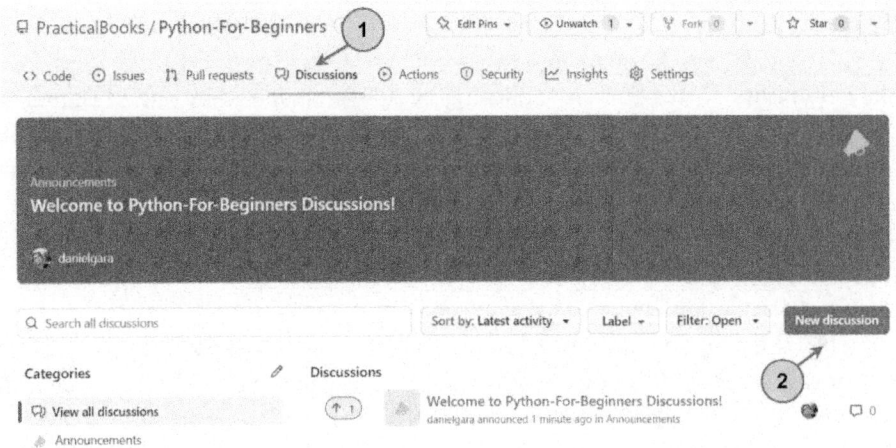

Figure 1-1. Discussion area of the book's repository.

In addition to using the book repository's discussion area, you can email your questions or suggestions to practicalbooksco@gmail.com. Please mention the book title in the subject of the message to be sent.

1.4. Cheat sheet

As an additional resource to the book, we have included a Python "Cheat Sheet" in the root directory of the book's repository, which you can find at https://github.com/PracticalBooks/Python-For-Beginners. This "Cheat Sheet" was created by the book's authors and includes many of the elements covered in this book.

We recommend that you download and take a look at the "Cheat Sheet." It consists of two images containing multiple code snippets organized by categories. You can download the first image from this link: https://github.com/PracticalBooks/Python-For-Beginners/blob/main/Cheat-Sheet-Part-1.png and the second image from this link: https://github.com/PracticalBooks/Python-For-Beginners/blob/main/Cheat-Sheet-Part-2.png.

These code snippets include various tricks (T01 to T85), and some have checkboxes that you can select or mark. At the end of most chapters in the book, you will find instructions on which tricks in the "Cheat Sheet" to mark, indicating the code snippets that have already been explained theoretically and practically (see Figure 1-2).

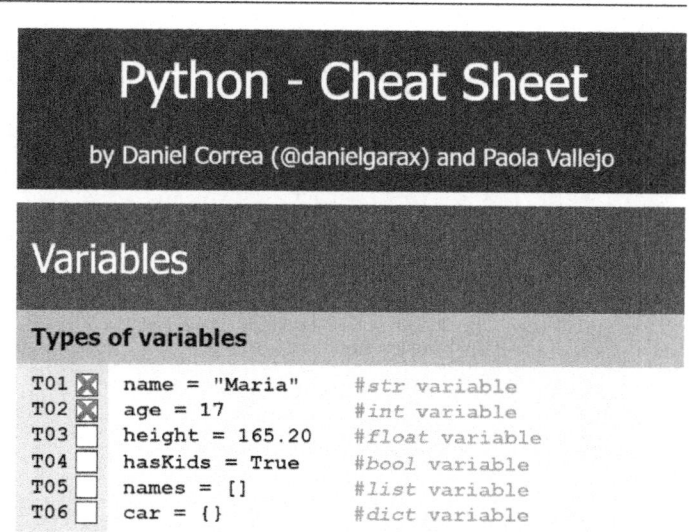
Figure 1-2. Excerpt of the Cheat Sheet, where the reader marks two seen tricks.

We recommend you print the "Cheat Sheet" and mark it with a pencil or pen. Or, if you prefer, download the image, and mark it digitally using programs such as "Paint", "Word", or any other. There are a total of 85 tricks or code snippets that you should understand by the end of this book.

Summary

This chapter introduced the book, including its structure and essential features created to facilitate reading and learning the elements that will be taught.

Now let's start our journey to the world of programming!

Chapter 02 – Computers and programming

What is a computer? What is programming? Is programming difficult? In this chapter, we will answer these fundamental questions and delve deeper into the programming world.

Next, we will cover the following sections:
1. Breaking myths.
2. Computers.
3. Programming languages.
4. Algorithms.

2.1. Breaking myths

Before starting to program and learn some key programming concepts, it is important to break some myths about programming and programmers (based on: *2020 - Sweigart, A. - Automate the boring stuff with Python, 2nd Edition*). So, let's look at some of these myths.

Should only software engineers or computer scientists learn how to program?

This is entirely false. In today's world, programming is a valuable skill anyone can benefit from learning, regardless of age, gender, or occupation. Many schools already teach programming at the secondary or even primary education level. Programming is everywhere, from smartphones and televisions to drones, cars, and washing machines. In addition, programming is used in everyday items such as traffic lights, advertising screens, and surveillance cameras.

Do programmers need to know a lot of math?

This is also false. Most programming does not require more math than basic arithmetic (addition, subtraction, multiplication, and division). Even if you don't know how to multiply or divide, if you can use a calculator or Google, you can develop many different types of programs.

Is learning to program difficult?

Nowadays, learning to program is much easier than before. Some programming languages have become simpler, and many resources are available, including videos, tutorials, books, and games, that accommodate different learning styles.

There are thousands of different resources for different tastes, such as videos on YouTube or TikTok, online tutorials, books, games, applications, and many others.

And as we mentioned earlier, in this book, we will guide you through the learning process step by step, explaining everything in detail without using complex examples. Once, Daniel's wife took an introductory programming course where the teacher presented examples with differential equations in the first class. So, we promise you won't find any differential equations on these pages!

Does programming only benefit me if I work as a programmer?

This is false. Suppose you are a lawyer. Should you then leave your profession as a lawyer and dedicate yourself to programming? Probably not. Suppose a lawyer has a case where they need to verify hundreds of physical documents and search for mentions of a particular medication. The lawyer could read each document one by one. Or the lawyer could scan the documents and write a small Python code that extracts the text from those documents and automatically searches for the name of the medication in them. The first option could take them days, weeks, or months. The second, just a few minutes.

Programming takes the lawyer's skills and amplifies them much more than their colleagues (it gives you a superpower).

If I learn to program, will I become a millionaire and buy my own Lambo (Lamborghini)?

We hope so. If that's the case, let us know, and hopefully, you'll invite the authors of this book for a ride in your Lambo. But let's look at some more realistic numbers (according to the US Bureau of Labor Statistics https://www.bls.gov/ooh/computer-and-information-technology/): (i) the average annual salary for various computer and programming-related occupations was $97,430, much higher than the annual average salary for all occupations ($45,760). And (ii) it is projected that computer and programming-related occupations will grow by 15% from 2021 to 2031, much faster than the average of all occupations.

TIP: If you need a little motivation about the importance of programming, we recommend watching the short YouTube video titled "Why Programming Is Important?". There, famous people from different professions discuss the importance of programming.

Now that we have broken some myths, let's start understanding the programming world a little better.

2.2. Computers

A **computer** is an electronic device that stores and processes data. We use computers for various tasks such as storing and editing photos, managing finances, playing games, and browsing the Internet.

We can manipulate a computer to do specific tasks for us. The problem is that computers cannot understand human language*. And that's why if we want to manipulate them to do something for us, we must speak a language they understand, known as a **programming language**.

***Note:** While virtual assistants such as Alexa or Siri can understand and execute voice commands, they are still limited in their abilities. For example, they may not be able to perform complex tasks such as analyzing hundreds of physical documents for searching a specific medication, as required by a lawyer. While AI-powered tools like Chat GPT have made significant advancements in this area, their responses are not always guaranteed to be accurate. While these tools can generate code, modifying them may require programming knowledge if they do not work as intended. Therefore, learning how to communicate with computers through programming languages is still necessary.

2.3. Programming languages

Programming is defining a series of instructions for the computer to do something for us. But, as we have seen, we should use a programming language to define those instructions.

There are different types of programming languages, but we can broadly categorize them into three main groups.

Machine language

This is the native language of a computer. Machine language instructions are written in binary code, which means they consist of ones and zeros. Figure 2-1 shows an example of a program written in machine language, which adds the numbers 1234 and 4321. This list of ones and zeros contains all the necessary commands and data to complete that task. The right column is a continuation of the left column (taken from: *1997 – Smith, S. W. – The scientist and engineer's guide to digital signal processing*).

```
10111001    00000000
11010010    10100001
00000100    00000000
10001001    00000000
00001110    10001011
00000000    00011110
00000000    00000010
10111001    00000000
11100001    00000011
00010000    11000011
10001001    10100011
00001110    00000100
00000010    00000000
```

Figure 2-1. Binary code representing the sum of two numbers (taken from *Smith, S. W.*).

Assembly language

Assembly language was a significant improvement over machine language as it made programming less error-prone and faster. It uses a set of mnemonics, which are short descriptive words representing the instructions. Then, those words and instructions are translated into machine language. However, one major limitation of assembly languages is that they depend on the machine's architecture, meaning that the code written on one machine may not work on another machine with different specifications. For example, the following code shows how to add the numbers 1234 and 4321 using assembly language (taken from: *1997 - Smith, S. W. - The scientist and engineer's guide to digital signal processing*).

Analyze

```
MOV CX,1234
MOV DS:[0],CX
MOV CX,4321
MOV DS:[2],CX
MOV AX,DS:[0]
MOV BX,DS:[2]
ADD AX,BX
MOV DS:[4],AX
```

High-level language

In the 1950s, a new generation of programming languages emerged known as "high-level languages." Unlike assembly languages, these languages are machine independent. It means that you can code your program and share it with your friends, and they can try it out without any problems on computers with different specifications than the computer on which it was developed. High-level languages are like English and are easier to learn and use. Usually, programming is taught in this type of language. Python, for example, is a high-level language. The following code shows how to add the numbers 1234 and 4321 using an instruction in a high-level language (in this case, Python).

Analyze

sum = 1234 + 4321

2.4. Algorithms

In this section, we will explore the concept of algorithms and their relationship with programming.

An **algorithm** is a precise set of instructions defining a procedure for solving a problem or performing a calculation. These instructions should be clear, unambiguous, and in a specific order. Algorithms can be designed using flowcharts, lists of steps, or pseudocode (a plain language description of the code to be developed). Finally, an algorithm can be implemented in different programming languages.

It's highly recommended to design an algorithm before starting to program, as it allows for a better understanding of the problem to be solved and the proposal of different solutions. This strategy can lead to more efficient and effective programming. Figure 2-2 shows an example of a strategy for working with algorithms.

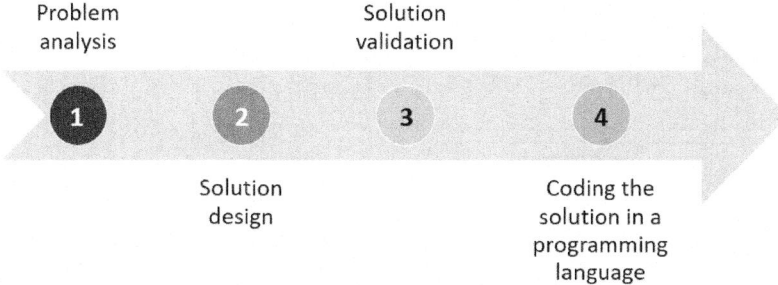

Figure 2-2. Strategy for working with algorithms.

Let's apply the strategy for working with algorithms with a specific example. Suppose we need to "calculate the average age of the four office workers".

1) Problem analysis

It consists of answering a series of questions applied to the problem to be solved or the calculation to be carried out. What is the objective? What are the input data? What calculations or processes must be carried out? What are the output data?

If we apply it to the office scenario, we will have the following:

Objective: To calculate the average age of the four office workers.
Input data: The age of worker 1, age of worker 2, age of worker 3, and age of worker 4.
Processes/calculations: Add the ages of workers 1, 2, 3, and 4. And then divide the sum by four.
Output data: The average age of the four office workers.

2) Solution design

After analyzing the problem, the next step is to design an algorithm that will solve the problem or perform the required calculation. The algorithm design can be represented in various ways, including flowcharts, step lists, or pseudocode.

Figure 2-3 shows two ways to represent the algorithm design that will serve as a basis for solving the previous problem.

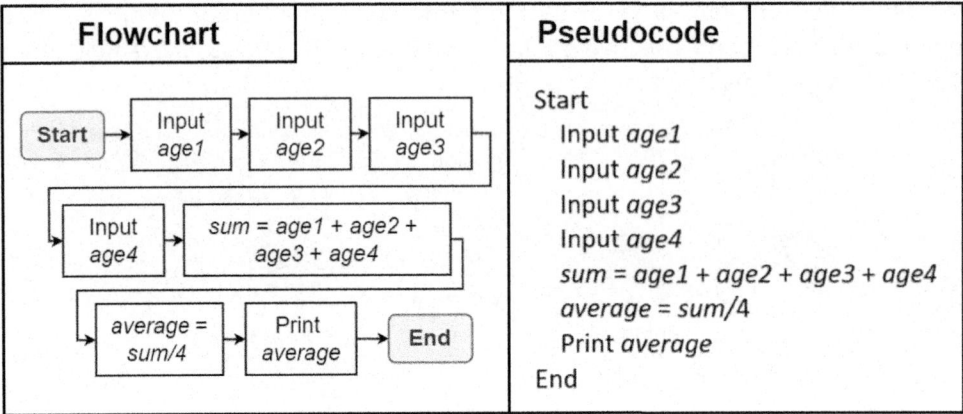

Figure 2-3. Flowchart and pseudocode of the exercise.

3) Solution validation

Solution validation involves testing the algorithm design to ensure its correctness. Various tools, including pen and paper, calculators, or Excel, can be used. For example, Figure 2-4 shows how Excel can be used to evaluate the algorithm.

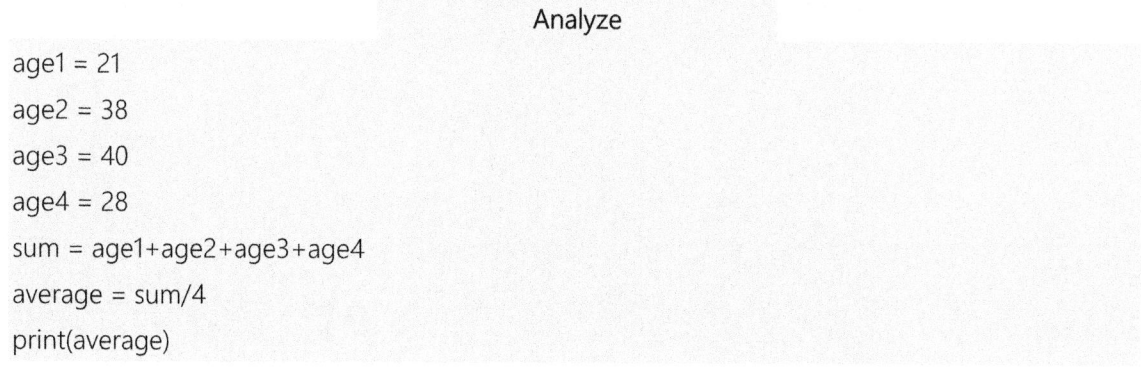

Figure 2-4. Validation of the algorithm in Excel.

4) Coding the solution in a programming language

After the algorithm design has been validated, the next step is to translate it into code in a programming language. Below is an example of the previous problem solved in Python. Figure 2-5 shows the execution of the code. For now, just analyze it. We will teach you how to code and evaluate these programs in upcoming chapters.

Analyze

```
age1 = 21
age2 = 38
age3 = 40
age4 = 28
sum = age1+age2+age3+age4
average = sum/4
print(average)
```

⤶ 31.75

Figure 2-5. Execution of the previous code.

Summary

In this chapter, we learned the fundamental elements of programming. We broke some myths about programming and learned basic concepts about computers, programming, programming languages, and algorithms.

In the next chapter, we will explain the basic concepts of Python.

Chapter 03 – Python

Python is one of the most popular and widely used programming languages worldwide. In this chapter, we will introduce Python and explore the different types of programs that can be developed using it.

Next, we will cover the following sections:
1. Introduction.
2. Comparing Python to other programming languages.
3. Types of programs that can be developed with Python.

3.1. Introduction

Python is a high-level programming language (https://www.python.org/) created in the late 1980s by Guido van Rossum. The name Python comes from the creator's affection for the British humor group "Monty Python," not the "snake" as is commonly believed.

Python has an open-source license, meaning that developers can modify, use, and redistribute its code for free without paying the original author.

Python is characterized as a friendly and easy-to-learn programming language.

3.2. Comparing Python to other programming languages

Many programmers use a platform called GitHub to manage and store the code of their programs. Every October, GitHub releases a report of the information collected from the site on a microsite called Octoverse (https://octoverse.github.com/). This microsite provides valuable insights into the millions of programmers who use the platform, including the most active regions, popular programming languages, and widely used open-source projects.

According to the Octoverse 2022 report, Python remains one of the most popular programming languages on the platform, as shown in Figure 3-1. Over the years, Python has consistently ranked among the top languages, and in 2022, it held the second position, behind only JavaScript.

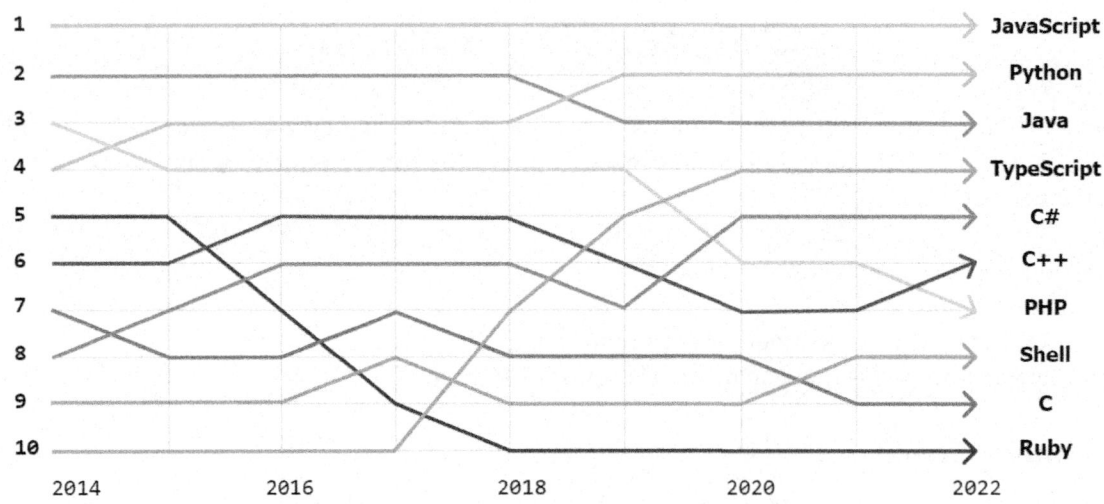
Figure 3-1. Top programming languages most used on GitHub in recent years.

But why is Python so popular for learning programming?

Let's compare it with Java by implementing a "Hello World" program, the simplest example you can find in any programming language. Its goal is to display the message "Hello World" on the computer screen.

To illustrate the comparison, let's first take a look at the following code that shows how to program a "Hello World" in Java.

Analyze

```
public class Principal {
  public static void main(String[] args) {
    System.out.println("Hello World");
  }
}
```

And let's take a look at the following code that shows how to program a "Hello World" in Python.

Analyze

```
print("Hello World")
```

Maybe now you understand why Python is considered a friendly and easy-to-learn language.

3.3. Types of programs that can be developed with Python

Python is a versatile language that allows developers to build a wide variety of applications. Python provides an open-source repository of packages called "PyPI," where programmers from worldwide contribute by developing different modules that can be reused to develop different types of applications. By using Python and some of these modules, we could:
- Develop web applications.
- Automate processes and activities through scripts.
- Perform data analysis.
- Develop video games.
- Extract data from the Internet through web scraping.
- Control IoT devices such as drones, embedded systems, or robots.
- Build computer vision applications such as image processing or face recognition.

It is just a tiny fraction of what Python can do. In fact, Python has been successfully used in various domains, from arts and aviation to e-commerce and bioinformatics. You can find many inspiring examples at https://www.python.org/about/success.

Summary

In this chapter, we have explored some fundamental aspects of Python, compared it to other programming languages, and introduced different types of applications you can build with Python and its packages.

In the next chapter, we will start coding with Python using a popular tool called Colab.

Chapter 04 – Hello world in Colab

There are many tools available for programming in Python. In this book, we will use Colab, a Google product that enables Python code programming from our browser. In this chapter, we will learn how to use Colab and create our initial programs.

Next, we will cover the following sections:
1. Introduction.
2. Colab activation.
3. "Hello World" in Colab.
4. Colab customization.

The code developed for this chapter is located at https://github.com/PracticalBooks/Python-For-Beginners/tree/main/Chapter04. We recommend that you develop the code by yourself to improve your coding skills. Then, in case of any issues, you can compare your code with the code available in the repository.

4.1. Introduction

There are several options available to develop Python code. For instance, one could download and install Python from its official website (https://www.python.org/downloads/) or use the Replit website to program online (https://replit.com/languages/python3), among other options. Each choice has its advantages and disadvantages.

In this book, we will use Google Colab or simply **Colab**, a tool created by Google that enables users to write and execute Python code in the browser without the need for installation. To use Colab, a Google account is required, and then Colab documents can be created on Google Drive for Python programming.

Compared to other tools, Colab offers several advantages, such as:
- **No program installation required:** To program with Colab, no installations are necessary. All that's required is an internet connection and a Google account.
- **Online data storage:** Since Colab connects to Google Drive, all the programs we create are automatically stored on the Internet (on Google Drive).
- **Easy code sharing:** Colab documents can be shared the same way as any other Google Document or Spreadsheet file, allowing for easy collaboration.

Next, we will guide you on how to activate Colab. However, first, please note that before proceeding, you need to create a Google account if you don't already have one. To create a Google account, please follow these steps: (1) go to https://www.google.com/account/about/, (2) click on "Create an account" (see Figure 4-1), and complete all the required steps and information.

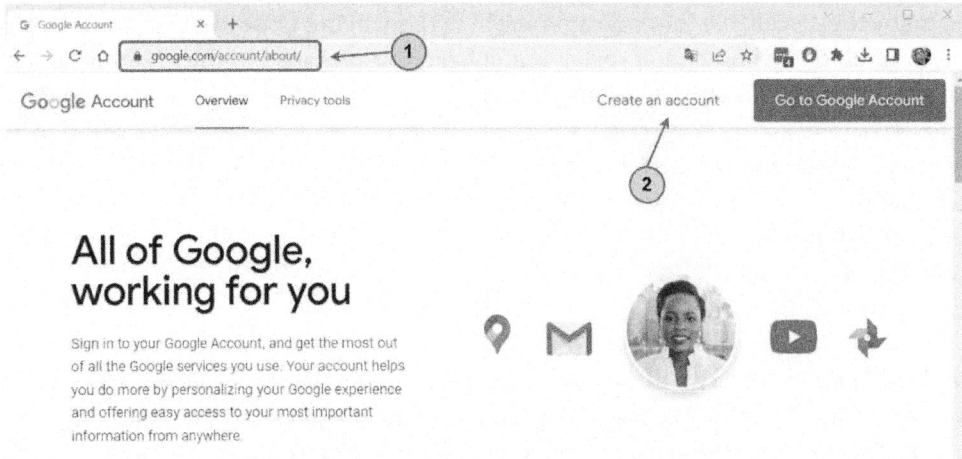

Figure 4-1. Website for creating a Google account.

4.2. Colab activation

Important note: The following steps and screenshots may vary slightly due to updates to the Google or Colab websites. If you encounter any issues with activating Colab, search for solutions on Google or leave a message in the "Discussion Zone" of the book's repository.

Next, complete the following steps to activate Colab with your Google account.

Step 1) Go to Google Drive (https://drive.google.com/drive/my-drive). Remember to sign in with your Google account (see Figure 4-2).

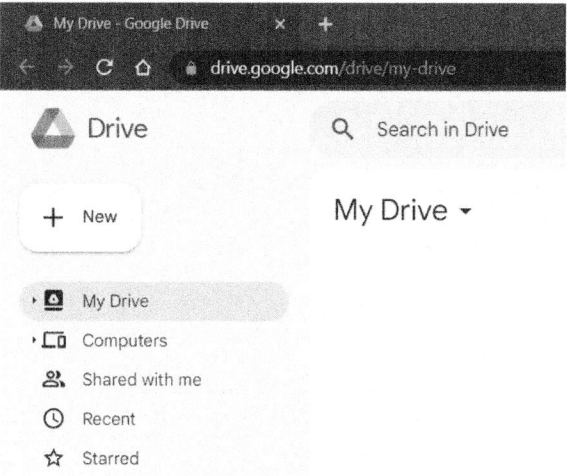
Figure 4-2. Accessing Google Drive.

Step 2) (1) Click on "+ New" in the top-left corner. (2) Click on "More" from the drop-down menu. (3) Click on "+ Connect more apps" (see Figure 4-3).

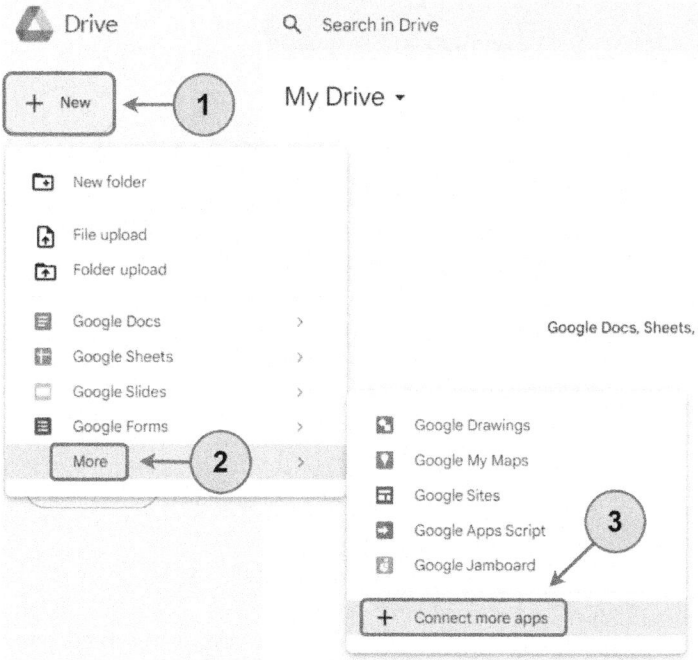
Figure 4-3. Connecting more apps to Google Drive.

Step 3) Once the pop-up window for the app store ("Google Workspace Marketplace") opens, (1) type "Colab" in the search bar at the top and press "Enter." Next, (2) click on "Colaboratory" (see Figure 4-4).

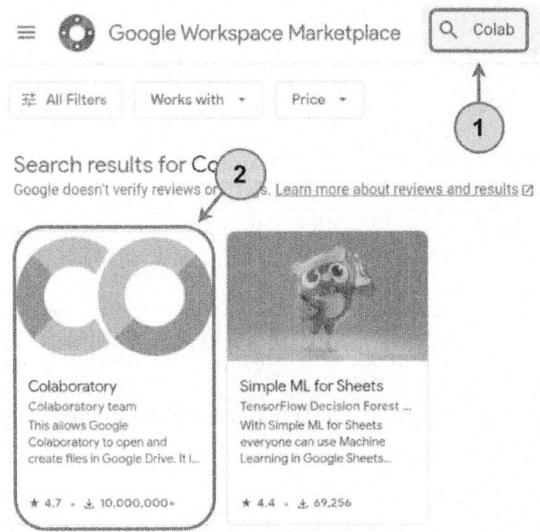

Figure 4-4. Searching for Google Colaboratory.

Step 4) Next, (1) click on "Install" (see Figure 4-5).

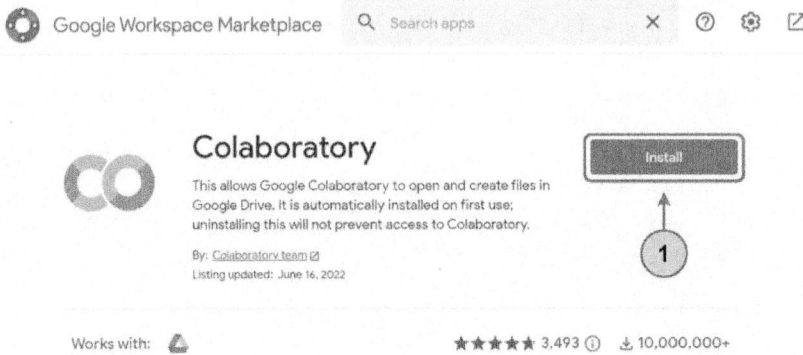

Figure 4-5. Installing Google Colaboratory.

Step 5) (1) Click on "Continue," and then (2) select the account in which you want to install and activate Colab (see Figure 4-6).

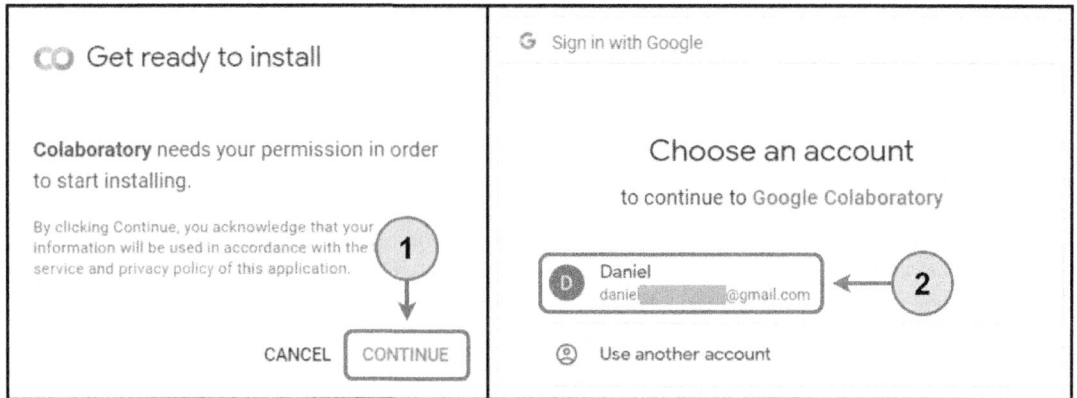

Figure 4-6. Granting permissions and associating the account with Colab.

Step 6) (1) Click on "Ok," and then (2) click on "Done" (see Figure 4-7). **Note:** sometimes, Google will require you to verify your account.

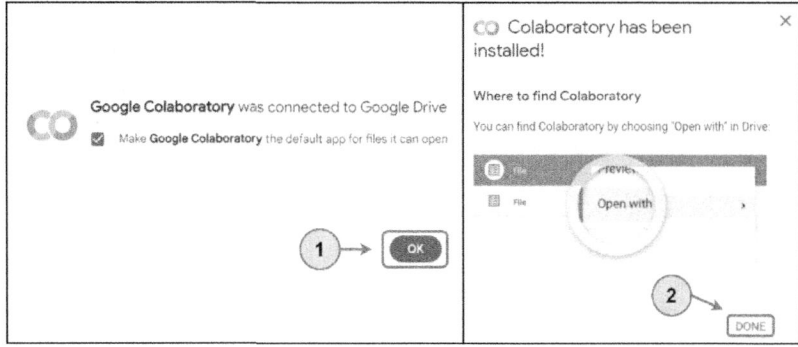

Figure 4-7. Accepting and finalizing connection with Colab.

Step 7) Finally, close the Google app store by clicking "X" in the top-right corner of the pop-up window.

You can now create Colab documents in your Google Drive account by completing the above steps. Next, we will create the first Colab document.

4.3. "Hello World" in Colab

To start coding in Python in Colab, you first need to create a Colab document by following the steps below.

Step 1) (1) Right-click on "My Drive," and then (2) click on "New folder." Next, (3) create a new folder named "Colab Files," and (4) click on "Create" (see Figure 4-8).

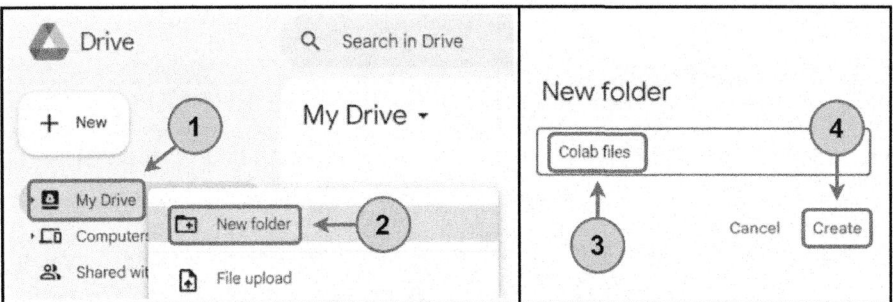

Figure 4-8. Creating a folder in Google Drive.

The "Colab files" folder will store all the code developed in this book.

Step 2) Double-click on the folder you just created to open it. Then, (1) while located in the "Colab files" folder, (2) click on "New". Next, (3) click on "More" and (4) click on "Google Colaboratory" (see Figure 4-9).

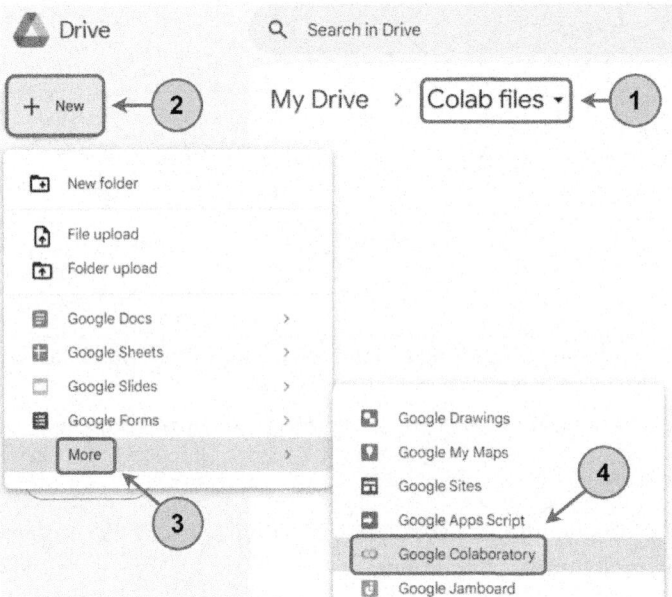

Figure 4-9. Creating a Colab document.

By following this process, you have created your first Colab document.

Step 3) After executing the previous step, a new tab will open with the Colab document. This Colab document is named "Untitled0.ipynb" by default. Now, double-click on "Untitled0.ipynb" and rename it to "C04-Hello-world-in-Colab.ipynb" (see Figure 4-10).

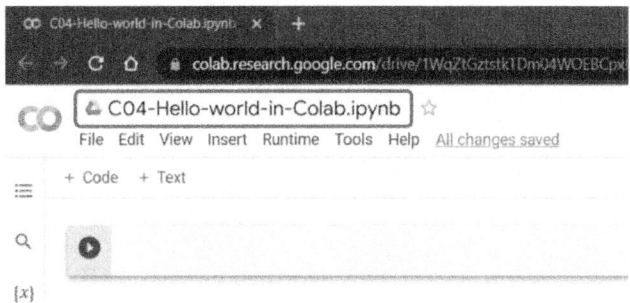

Figure 4-10. Renaming a Colab document.

For each chapter of this book, it is recommended that you create a new Colab document where you program the codes and exercises presented.

Step 4) Now, create your first text cell. First, (1) Click on "+ Text". Then, (2) Write "Our first code - Hello World". Finally, (3) click on the up arrow "↑" to move the text cell above the code cell (see Figure 4-11). Later, we will show you how to add a code cell.

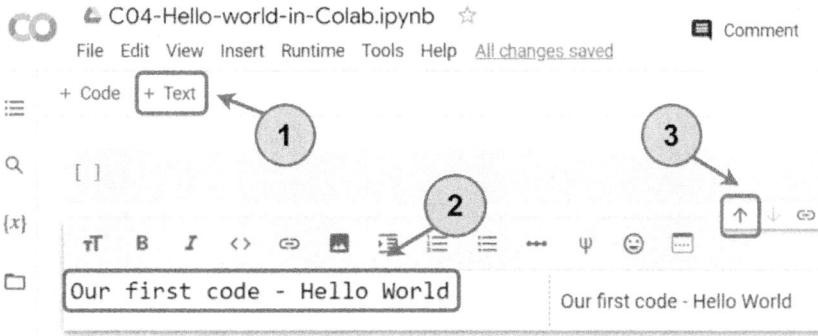

Figure 4-11. Creating a text cell in Colab.

Adding notes before code is very useful to easily remember what we are programming. It is another advantage of Colab compared to other similar tools.

Step 5) Now click on the gray area below our text cell (code cell) and type *print("Hello World")* inside it (see Figure 4-12).

Figure 4-12. Programming a "Hello World" code in Colab.

Step 6) Finally, (1) click on the white arrow with a black background "▷" to execute the previous code cell. (2) You should see the result of the execution below the code area. This process may take a few seconds (see Figure 4-13).

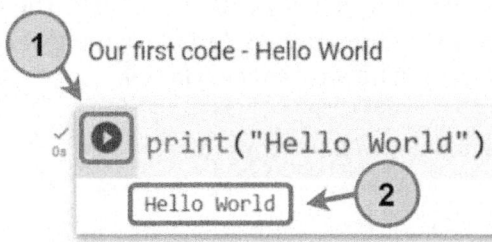

Figure 4-13. Executing a code cell in Colab.

Congratulations, you have just programmed and executed your first Python code.

4.4. Colab customization

Before making a couple of customizations, let's practice using Colab on the current document.

Create a new text cell (by clicking on "+ Text") and write the following message: "Multiple Hello World". Then create a new code cell (by clicking on "+ Code") and add the following code:

Code and execute

```
print("Hello World")
print("Hello World")
print("Hello World")
```

The new sections should appear as shown in Figure 4-14.

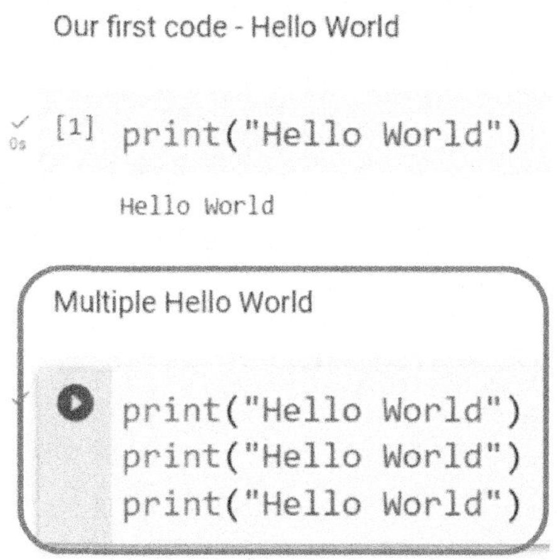

Our first code - Hello World

```
[1] print("Hello World")
    Hello World
```

```
Multiple Hello World

▶ print("Hello World")
  print("Hello World")
  print("Hello World")
```

Figure 4-14. Adding cells to a Colab document.

Now, execute the above code, and the text "Hello World" should appear three times on the screen.

The problem with the previous output is that as we add more lines of code, it becomes harder to identify which line number corresponds to which instruction. So, let's make minor customization in Colab.

(1) Click on "Tools", (2) then click on "Settings", (3) then click on "Editor", and (4) select the options: (i) "Show line numbers" and (ii) "Show indentation guides". Finally, (5) click on "Save" (see Figure 4-15).

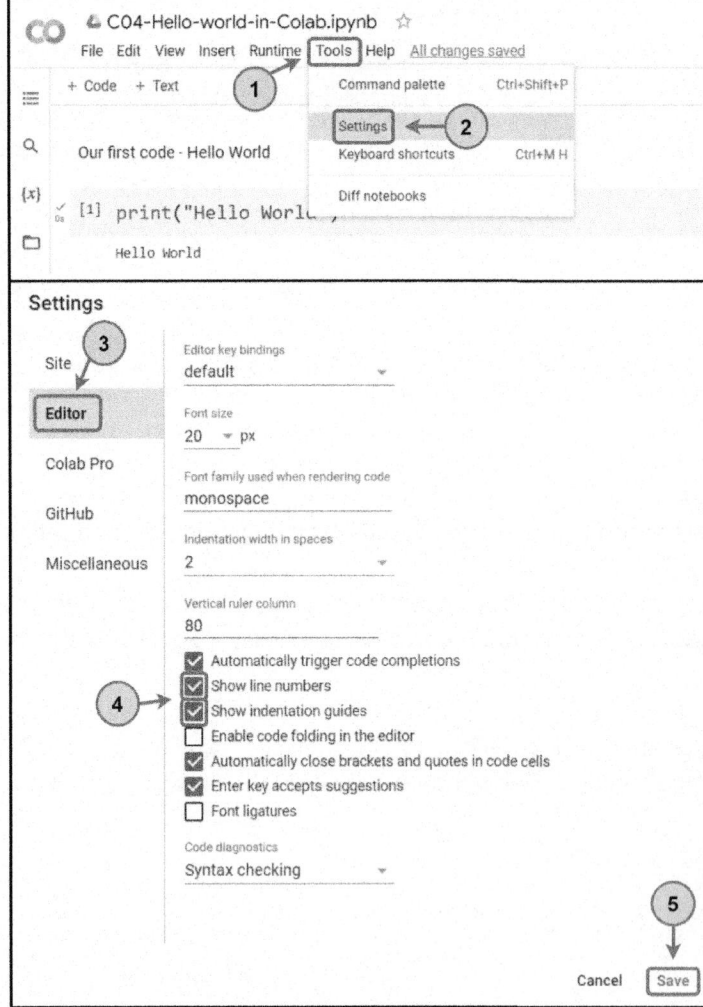

Figure 4-15. Colab customization.

Enabling the above options will make it easier to read the developed code.

Python version

Programming languages evolve, introducing new versions with new options and functionalities. Similarly, Colab regularly updates its Python version. At the time of writing, Colab is using version 3.9.16 of Python. To check the current Python version, you can execute the code shown in Figure 4-16.

Figure 4-16. Check the Python version in Colab.

Critical errors in Colab

Before concluding this chapter, let's discuss one last suggestion regarding Colab. **Please pay close attention to this tip, as it will be crucial if your developed codes stop working mysteriously.**

Every time a code cell is executed in Colab, the code data is stored in the memory of something called "runtime". A runtime is a virtual machine that Colab allocates to you. Sometimes, due to errors in the programming logic, the stored data in the runtime memory can cause problems. For example, in Figure 4-17, you can see that we tried to execute the *print("Hello World")* code and received an error. Although the code looks fine, we intentionally introduced a bug in another code cell that changed the meaning of *print* in our current runtime memory.

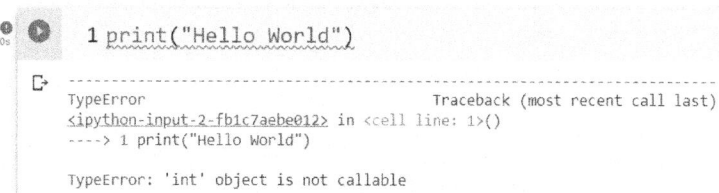

Figure 4-17. Code cell error in Colab.

If this happens to you and you see code that should theoretically work but doesn't, the solution is simple. First, (1) click on "Runtime," then (2) click on "Restart runtime" (see Figure 4-18). Finally, click on "Yes" to allocate a new fresh runtime.

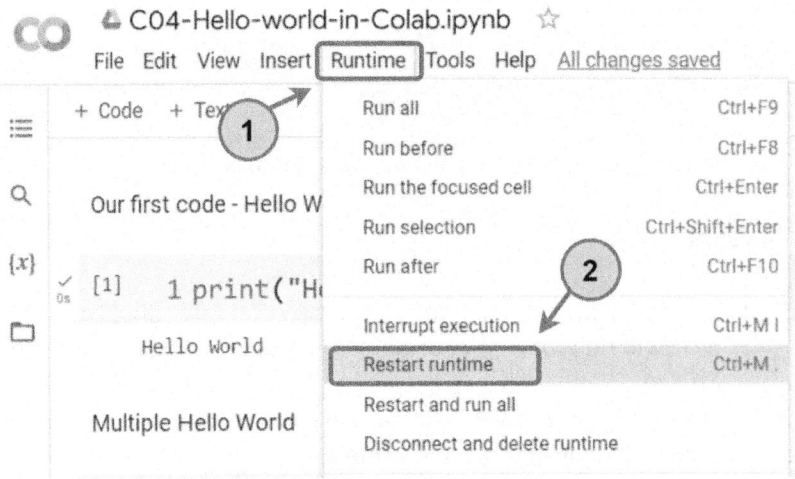

Figure 4-18. Restart runtime in Colab.

Summary

In this chapter, we learned how to use Colab, link our Google Drive account with Colab, create Colab documents, create and define text and code cells in Colab, program and execute code in Colab, and customize the appearance of our Colab documents.

In the next chapter, we will learn how to manipulate three types of variables in Python, one of the fundamental programming concepts.

Chapter 05 – Int, float, and str variables

Variables are fundamental elements in Python and many other programming languages. It is because variables store the values (data) in our programs. In this chapter, we will explain how variables work and introduce some of the main types of variables.

Next, we will cover the following sections:
1. Variables.
2. Creating variables.
3. Variable types.
4. Printing variables.
5. Modifying variables.
6. The type function.
7. Comments in Python.
8. Exercises.

The code developed for this chapter is located at https://github.com/PracticalBooks/Python-For-Beginners/tree/main/Chapter05. We recommend that you develop the code by yourself to improve your coding skills. Then, in case of any issues, you can compare your code with the code available in the repository.

Remember that we suggest you create a new Colab document for each book chapter. It will allow you to keep your codes organized.

5.1. Variables

A **variable** is a reserved space in the computer's memory where we store a value. In Python, we create a variable using the following syntax (we will explain this process step by step in the next section). For example, the following code creates a variable "age" with a value of 21:

Code

age = 21

When we create the variable *age*, the computer reserves a space in its memory to store the value of this variable (in this case, the number *21*).

In this book, we will imagine variables as "boxes" that contain two labels and a piece of paper. For example, Figure 5-1 graphically represents the variable *age*.

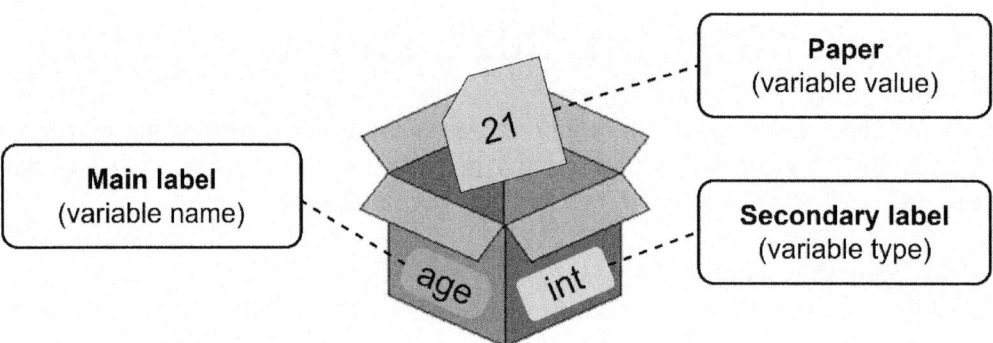

Figure 5-1. Graphical representation of a variable.

The above box contains the following:
- **Variable name:** This is the main label of the box (located on the bottom left side of the box). We choose the name ourselves, and it should be descriptive enough to help us to remember what we are storing in the box.
- **Variable value:** This is the piece of paper stored inside the box. We define the value ourselves depending on what we want to store.
- **Variable type:** This is the secondary label of the box (located on the bottom right side of the box). Python dynamically assigns the type based on the value we assign to the variable. In this case, Python assigns it an *int* (integer) type since we are storing the number *21* (later, we will see different variable types).

As we develop more complex programs, we may use hundreds or thousands of variables to store different types of information. Therefore, understanding how to create and use variables is an essential skill for any programmer.

5.2. Creating variables

In the previous section, we created our first variable. Now, we'll explain the process of creating a variable in detail. To create a variable in Python, we use the following structure:

Analyze structure

variableName = variableValue

The structure above consists of three parts:
- First, we must **give the variable a name**. The name can be defined using letters and numbers without using spaces. We should define names that make it easy to remember what we're storing there.

- Next, we must use the "=" operator. It is an **assignment operator** that assigns the value on the right to the variable on the left.
- Finally, on the right side, we place **the value we want to store** in the variable.

Rules for naming variables

Let's look at some rules for naming variables:
- **Use only letters, numbers, and underscores:** Avoid using spaces, special characters, or punctuation marks. Using any other character will result in an error.
- **Start with a letter or an underscore:** It cannot start with a number.
- **Avoid using reserved keywords:** Python has reserved keywords that have specific meanings and are used to define the language's syntax. For example, you cannot use *if*, *while*, or *for* as variable names (we'll explain some of these reserved keywords later).

As we learned earlier, giving appropriate names to variables is crucial for making our code and programs understandable.

Quick discussion: Let's see the importance of good variable naming with these two quotes from the book (*2019 - Thomas, D., & Hunt, A. - The Pragmatic Programmer: your journey to mastery*). (i) *The beginning of wisdom is to call things by their proper name. - Confucius.* (ii) *Why is naming important? Because good names make code easier to read, and you have to read it to change it.*

In addition to choosing appropriate names for variables, it's also highly recommended to use a consistent naming style.

TIP: When defining variables, always use the same naming convention. In this book, we'll use camelCase. **camelCase** is a writing style that involves joining two or more words without spaces between them but differentiating them with an initial uppercase letter from the second word onwards. For example, if we want to define a variable that stores "my first name," we can call it *myFirstName*.

5.3. Variable types

So far, we have only created a variable of type *int* (integer). However, the programs we use daily are not only composed of integers. Let's analyze three common types of variables in Python.

***str* variables (string)**
They are created as texts or characters between double or single quotes. For example: "Hello", "House", "Happy birthday", and 'I have 3 sisters'.

***int* variables (integer):**
They are created as numbers that do not contain decimal places. For example: -6, 1, 10, 25.

***float* variables (floating point):**
They are created as numbers that contain decimal places. For example: -1.25, 1.0, 1.25.

In the following code, we see the creation of three variables with different types. Also, in Figure 5-2, we see the graphical representation of these variables.

Code

```
name = "Maria"
age = 21
height = 164.1
```

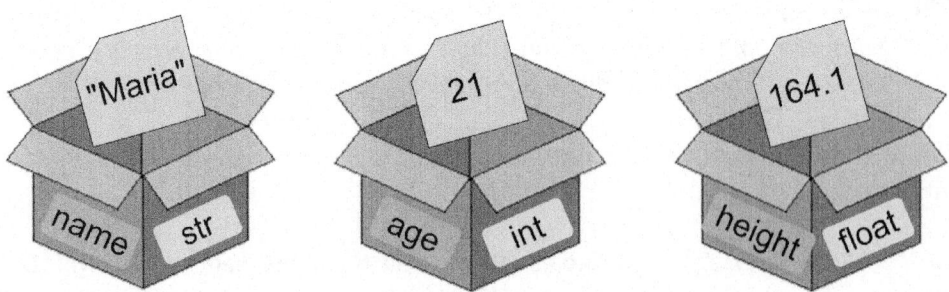

Figure 5-2. Graphical representation of variables with different types.

5.4. Printing variables

So far, we have created variables but haven't used them in our programs yet. One common task is to print the contents of these variables on the screen. Let's code and execute the following code.

Code and execute

```
name = "Maria"
age = 21
height = 164.1

print(name)
print(age)
print(height)
```

We use the *print* function in the last three lines of the above code. The **print** function allows us to display information on the screen. In this case, we pass the name of each variable between the parenthesis of the *print* function. When we execute the code above (see Figure 5-3), it will display the value stored in the name variable (which is *"Maria"*), followed by the value stored in the age variable (which is *21*), and finally, the value stored in the height variable (which is *164.1*).

```
⤷  Maria
    21
    164.1
```

Figure 5-3. Execution of the previous code.

Quick discussion: The values we pass between parentheses to functions are called arguments. An **argument** is a value that the function receives to perform actions. In the previous example, we passed arguments to the *print()* function, and the value of each argument was displayed on the screen. We will discuss the topic of functions and arguments in detail in Chapter 14.

Finally, let's analyze the following code:

Code and execute

```
age = 21
print(agee)
```

When we execute the above code, an error will appear on the screen (see Figure 5-4), indicating that the variable *agee* is not defined. The problem is that the variable name contains an extra letter "e". In Python, we must be very careful when using variable names, as the name must be exactly the same in every line of code where we use the variable. Python even distinguishes between uppercase and lowercase letters.

```
NameError                                 Traceback (most recent call last)
<ipython-input-2-43f79bfa7606> in <cell line: 2>()
      1 age = 21
----> 2 print(agee)

NameError: name 'agee' is not defined
```

Figure 5-4. Error when using an undefined variable.

5.5. Modifying Variables

As their name implies, variables can change their values. For example, we can create a variable to store the price of a product and then modify that price in the code (e.g., to apply a discount).

Modifying the value of a variable

The following code shows how we create a variable named *productPrice*, print its contents, modify its value, and print its contents again. Note that the numbers on the left-hand side of the code are there only to help us easily identify the lines of code and **should not be included in your code**.

Code and execute

1. productPrice = 150
2. print(productPrice)
3. productPrice = 250
4. print(productPrice)

Figure 5-5 shows what happens internally in the computer's memory. **Lines 1 to 4 are executed in sequence**. When line 1 is executed, a variable named *productPrice* is created with a value of *150*. Later, when line 3 is executed, the value of the *productPrice* variable is modified from *150* to *250*. Since the variables have the same name, Python only reserves one space in memory (i.e., **it only creates one box**).

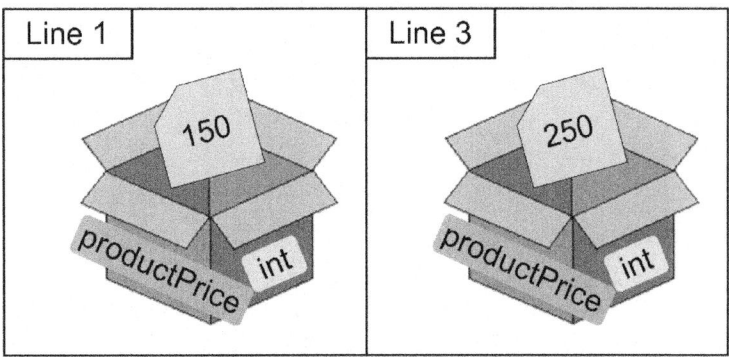

Figure 5-5. Modifying the value of a variable.

Modifying the value and type of a variable

In Python, it is possible to modify both the value and type of a variable. The following code shows how we create a variable named *productPrice* (initially with an *int* value), print its contents, then modify its value (to a *float* value), and print its contents again.

Code and execute

1. productPrice = 150
2. print(productPrice)
3. productPrice = 250.5
4. print(productPrice)

Figure 5-6 shows what happens internally in the computer's memory. When line 1 is executed, the variable *productPrice* is created with a value of *150* and an *int* type. Then, line 3 is executed, its value is modified to *250.5*, which also changes its type to *float*.

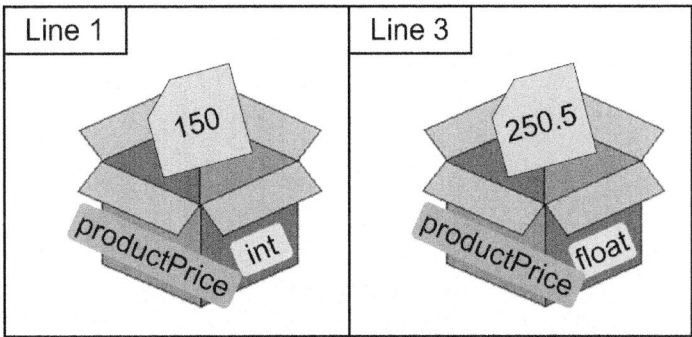

Figure 5-6. Modifying the value and type of a variable.

**Quick discussion:** Recognizing that variables in Python handle different types will help us better understand how Python works and our different possibilities for using those variables. Other programming languages have stricter typing (for example, Java). In Java, an *int* variable could not be modified to a *float* number (it could only be modified to another *int* number).

Reusing variables to define new variables

In many programming languages, it is possible to create or modify variables based on the values of previously created variables. The following code shows how: (i) we create a variable *luisAge* with a value of *10*, (ii) we create a variable *lauraAge* with a value of *20*, (iii) we create a variable *sum* that will be equal to the value contained in the variable *luisAge* plus the value contained in the variable *lauraAge* (which is *30*), (iv) we create a variable *average* that will be equal to the variable *sum* divided by 2, and (v) we print the value stored in *average* (*15.0*).

Code and execute

1. luisAge = 10
2. lauraAge = 20
3. sum = luisAge + lauraAge
4. average = sum/2
5. print(average)

Figure 5-7 shows the output on the screen when running the above code. As we can see, the result is *15.0*, which means that *average* is of type *float*. It is because division in Python always generates a *float* type (regardless of the type of the numbers being divided).

⇥ 15.0

Figure 5-7. Execution of the previous code.

5.6. The type function

In the previous sections, we identified the types of variables by imagining how they are stored in memory. However, Python offers a built-in function called *type* that allows us to identify the type of each variable. The **type** function takes the name of a variable as an argument and returns its type (we will cover functions, arguments, and return values in Chapter 14). Then, we can use the *print* function to print the types of those variables on the screen.

The following code shows the creation of the variable *productPrice* and then prints the defined type of that variable (which is initially an *int* type). Then, the variable is modified with a float value, and the variable type is printed again (this time *float* type). Figure 5-8 shows the output on the screen when running this code.

Code and execute

1. productPrice = 150
2. print(**type**(productPrice))
3. productPrice = 250.5
4. print(**type**(productPrice))

```
<class 'int'>
<class 'float'>
```

Figure 5-8. Execution of the previous code.

5.7. Comments in Python

Many programming languages allow adding comments to the code we are developing. These comments are defined to leave clues about what the code does. These clues can be for my "future self" (for example, if I return to the project in two weeks or two months and need to quickly remember what that piece of code did) or for colleagues to understand my code.

The following code shows two ways to define comments in Python. Line 1 shows how to define **single-line comments** (using the hashtag symbol "#"). If a line of code in Python starts with "#", Python will ignore it (will not execute it). Lines 4 to 5 show how to define **multiline comments** (using three double quotes """). Python will ignore all lines starting with three double quotes until it finds another set of three double quotes representing the end of the comment.

Code and execute

1. # The following line represents the monthly salary of a person
2. salary = 5000
3.
4. """ We will divide the salary by 2 to distribute it among the family
5. members and print the result to the screen """
6. print(salary/2)

5.8. Exercises

Theoretical exercises

E5.1. What type is each of the following variables?

Analyze

1. totalToPay = 1450.7
2. productName = "iPhone 14"
3. satellites = 7
4. engines = "4"

E5.2. What is the purpose of the *print* function?

E5.3. Which of the following lines of code presents an incorrect way to define a variable?

Analyze

1. cat age = 7
2. my_email = "test@gmail.com"
3. duplicatedEmail = my_email

Practical exercises

E5.4. Write a program in which you create four variables: one that contains your first name, another for your last name, another for your age, and another for your height. And finally, print the content of each variable to the screen. **Note:** use the type that you consider most appropriate for each variable.

Summary

In this chapter, we learned how to create and manipulate variables in Python. We imagined variables as boxes that contain a name, a type, and a value. We learned about three fundamental variable types (*int*, *float*, and *str*). We learned that variables could be modified by changing their value, type, or both. We discovered that *print* is used to print data to the screen, *type* is used to return the variable type, and we learned two ways to define comments in Python.

**Cheat Sheet:** Now, we will take the Cheat Sheet and mark the tricks related to the topics learned in this chapter. Mark the following tricks with an "X": T01, T02, T03, T07, T08, T09, T10, and T11.

Figure 5-9 shows an excerpt from the cheat sheet, in which the tricks learned so far are marked.

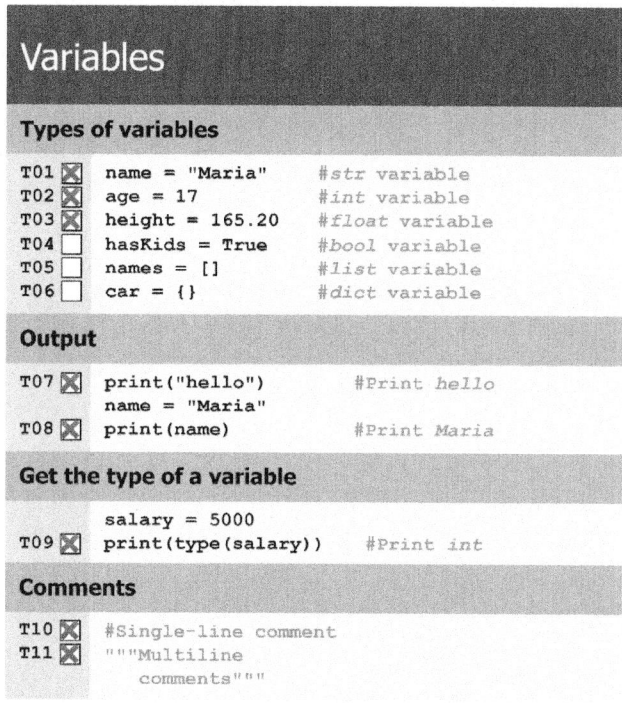

Figure 5-9. Excerpt from the Cheat Sheet, where the reader marks the tricks seen in this chapter.

In the next chapter, we will continue printing information on the screen (output) and learn how to input our data into the program (input).

Chapter 06 – Data input and output

Many of the programs we use daily are interactive, requiring us as users to input information via forms, voice commands, videos, and more. Based on this input, the programs generate responses, which can be displayed on our screens as printed messages, audio, video, text messages, and so on.

In this chapter, we will learn how to input data using the keyboard (**input**) and how programs display results on our computer screens (**output**).

Next, we will cover the following sections:
1. Keyboard input of data.
2. Conversion of variable types.
3. The print function.
4. Concatenation of data on screen output.
5. Exercises.

The code developed for this chapter is located at https://github.com/PracticalBooks/Python-For-Beginners/tree/main/Chapter06. We recommend that you develop the code by yourself to improve your coding skills. Then, in case of any issues, you can compare your code with the code available in the repository.

Remember that we suggest you create a new Colab document for each book chapter. It will allow you to keep your codes organized.

6.1. Keyboard input of data

In this book, our primary focus will be collecting information through the keyboard of the device used for programming. It's common for programs to require keyboard input for various types of data, such as a user's name, age, salary, email address, or even the course grade.

The *input* function

In Python, the ***input*** function allows you to capture information through the user's keyboard input. When this function is coded, the program waits for the user to enter data through the keyboard and then press *Enter*. The collected information is usually assigned to a variable. The information will be stored as an *str* data type regardless of what the user enters via keyboard.

Line 2 of the following code shows how to use the *input* function. When the code is executed, the program will display the message on line 1. Then, on line 2, it will wait for the user to input information through the keyboard. After the user enters the information and presses *Enter*, the *input* function will capture the value entered and assign it to the variable *name* (remember, the variable type will be *str* by default). Then, on line 3, a message will be printed, and on line 4, the value stored in the *name* variable will be printed. Figure 6-1 shows the execution of line 2.

Code and execute

1. print("Enter your name: ")
2. name = **input()**
3. print("Your name is: ")
4. print(name)

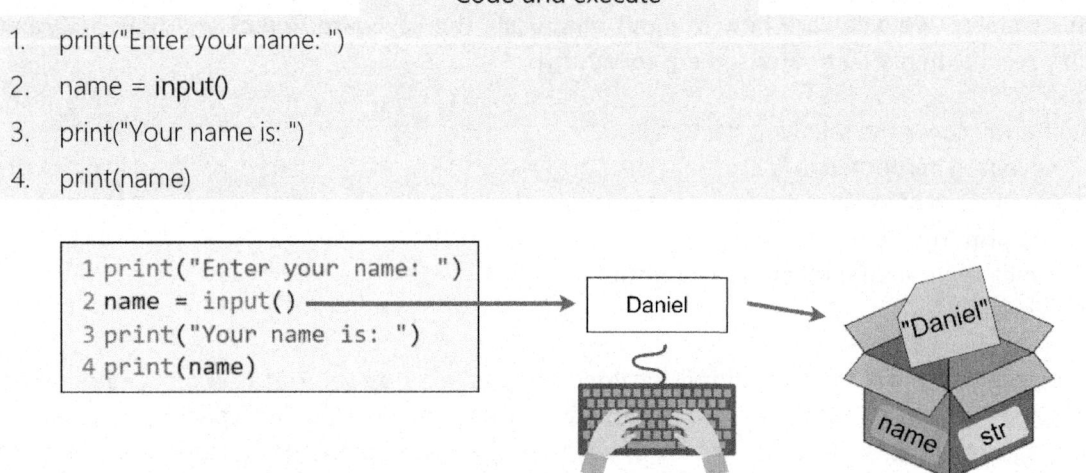

Figure 6-1. Graphical representation of the *input* function in the previous code.

input function – default data type

By default, whatever the user enters through the keyboard after calling the *input* function will be type *str* (text). It doesn't matter if the input is a number or a decimal; it will still be defined as an *str* (text) type.

The following code shows a program in which, on line 1, a person's age is entered via keyboard. That age is stored in the variable *age*. Note that on line 1, we are sending an argument (a text) to the *input* function. This argument is optional, but when sent, the *input* function will print the value of the received argument (in this case, it will print "Enter your age:"). Then, line 2 will calculate half of the age received by dividing the variable *age* by 2 (and assigning the result to the variable *halfAge*). Finally, on line 3, the program will print the value stored in the variable *halfAge*.

However, as shown in Figure 6-2, the code will display an error indicating that an *str* value (referring to the *age* variable) cannot be divided by an *int* value (referring to the number *2*) because in Python, dividing a text by an integer is impossible. Additionally, we have confirmed that the *input* function always returns an *str* variable (regardless of whether we enter a number).

Code and execute

1. age = input("Enter your age: ")
2. halfAge = age/2
3. print(halfAge)

```
Enter your age: 21
-------------------------------------------------------------------------
TypeError                                  Traceback (most recent call last)
<ipython-input-1-701f7f8e0dc3> in <cell line: 2>()
      1 age = input("Enter your age: ")
----> 2 halfAge = age/2
      3 print(halfAge)

TypeError: unsupported operand type(s) for /: 'str' and 'int'
```
Figure 6-2. Execution of the previous code.

To solve the previous problem, we need to perform a type conversion, which will be explained in the next section.

TIP: Often, we spend a lot of time trying to make our code work without analyzing the obvious – "Read the damn error message" (quoted from: *2019 - Thomas, D., & Hunt, A. - The Pragmatic Programmer: your journey to mastery*).

6.2. Conversion of variables types

The conversion of variable types is a common process in programming. Sometimes, we will receive information from the user as input that we need to convert to *int* or *float* data types. Other times, we may need to convert numbers to text to store information in plain text files (txt) or comma-separated value files (CSV), among others.

int, *float*, and *str* functions

The **int** function allows us to convert a number or a text to *int* type.
The **float** function allows us to convert a number or text to *float* type.
The **str** function allows us to convert a value to *str* type.

To all of the above functions, we must pass the value to convert in parentheses (as an argument). The value passed as an argument must be a valid value to convert. For example, we can execute the code *int("3")* since the text sent as an argument contains a valid value to convert to *int*.

However, we cannot execute *int("Hello")* since *"Hello"* cannot be represented numerically and, therefore, cannot be converted to *int*.

The following code shows how to correct the code to "calculate half of the age" so that it does not throw an error. In this case, we use the *int* function to convert the value collected by the *input* function to *int* type. In this case, line 2 can be executed since it will perform a division between *int* values, which is valid. And finally, half of the age will be calculated and printed (see execution in Figure 6-3).

Code and execute

1. age = **int**(input("Enter your age: "))
2. halfAge = age/2
3. print(halfAge)

```
Enter your age: 21
10.5
```

Figure 6-3. Execution of the previous code.

The following code shows the differences when converting values received by the *input* function into different data types. Line 1 shows how to receive the father's age from the keyboard (as there is no conversion, the variable *fatherAge* will be of type *str*). Line 2 shows how to receive the mother's age from the keyboard (as there is a conversion, the variable *motherAge* will be of type *int*). Line 3 shows how to receive the father's height from the keyboard (as there is a conversion, the variable *fatherHeight* will be of type *float*). Finally, the type and value of each variable are printed on the screen (see Figure 6-4).

Code and execute

1. fatherAge = input("Enter age: ")
2. motherAge = int(input("Enter age: "))
3. fatherHeight = float(input("Enter height: "))
4. print(type(fatherAge))
5. print(type(motherAge))
6. print(type(fatherHeight))
7. print(fatherAge)
8. print(motherAge)
9. print(fatherHeight)

```
Enter age: 30
Enter age: 29
Enter height: 179.3
<class 'str'>
<class 'int'>
<class 'float'>
30
29
179.3
```

Figure 6-4. Execution of the previous code.

Figure 6-5 shows the graphical representation of the variables previously created in the code.

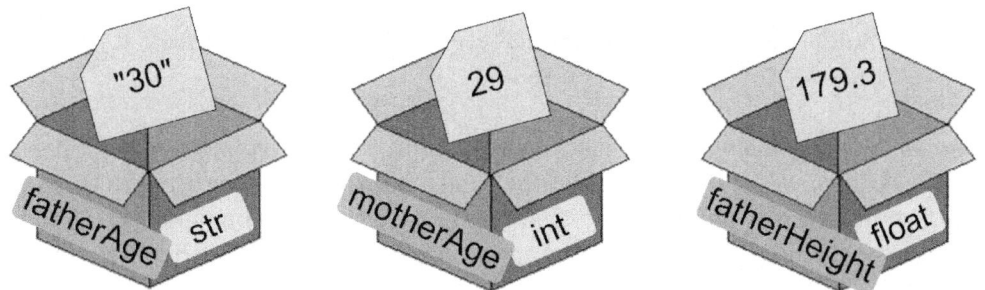

Figure 6-5. Graphical representation of the variables of the previous code.

6.3. The print function

So far, we have used the *print* function multiple times. The *print* function will be the most commonly used mechanism in this book to display information or program results. The *print* function takes an argument, either text or a variable, and displays it on the screen.

The following code shows how we create and display a couple of variables on the screen. Lines 3 and 5 show how to use the *print* function to display text values on the screen, while lines 4 and 6 show how to use the *print* function to display values contained within variables. Both cases are valid in Python.

Code and execute

1. name = "Paola"
2. age = 30
3. print("Name: ")
4. print(name)
5. print("Age: ")
6. print(age)

The previous code presents an issue. When we have many variables and texts, we would have to define dozens of lines of code to print on the screen, one by one, each value and variable. In the next section, we will see how to solve this problem.

6.4. Concatenation of data on screen output

Concatenating multiple outputs and values (that are related) into a single *print* statement is very convenient for reducing the number of code lines.

In Python, we can use a single *print* statement to print multiple values and multiple variable contents. To do this, we use the "+" operator, which allows us to **concatenate** (join) multiple strings. Sometimes we may need to use the *str* function (to convert a numerical value to type *str*) to perform the above process. Since in Python, we cannot concatenate a string with a number.

The following code shows how to perform the concatenation process. Line 3 uses the "+" operator to concatenate the text *"Name:"* with the variable *productName* of type *str*. This concatenation is valid because both values are *str*. However, the code will fail when executing line 4 because, in this line, we use the "+" operator to concatenate the text *"Price:"* with the variable *productPrice* of type *int*. Since Python does not allow concatenating texts with numbers, the program, when executed, will display an error on the screen (see Figure 6-6).

Code and execute

1. productName = "Chromecast"
2. productPrice = 30
3. print("Name: "+productName)
4. print("Price: "+productPrice)

```
Name: Chromecast
-----------------------------------------------------------------------
TypeError                                 Traceback (most recent call last)
<ipython-input-5-c205329c58a4> in <cell line: 4>()
      2 productPrice = 30
      3 print("Name: "+productName)
----> 4 print("Price: "+productPrice)

TypeError: can only concatenate str (not "int") to str
```

Figure 6-6. Error when trying to concatenate invalid types.

To solve the previous problem, we must convert the numeric value to type *str*. The following code shows how in line 4, we use the *str* function to convert the value stored in the variable *productPrice* to type *str*, and now the concatenation is valid. Figure 6-7 shows the output on the screen of the execution of the previous code.

Code and execute

1. productName = "Chromecast"
2. productPrice = 30
3. print("Name: "+productName)
4. print("Price: "+**str**(productPrice))

```
Name: Chromecast
Price: 30
```

Figure 6-7. Execution of the previous code.

Quick discussion: In Python, it is also possible to print multiple values and variables within a single *print* statement by separating them with commas "," (as shown in the following code). In this case, the values separated by commas can be of different types (there is no need to convert them all to *str*). We can see that we do not need to convert *productPrice* to *str*. However, in this book, we will only use concatenation since repeating this process helps us internalize the concept of variable typing in Python. This will be very useful for understanding later concepts.

Code and execute

1. productName = "Chromecast"
2. productPrice = 30
3. print("Name:",productName,"- Price:",productPrice)

6.5. Exercises

Theoretical exercises

E6.1. What type is each of the following variables? **Note:** assume that in line 2, the user enters 59.

Analyze

1. elonAge = 51
2. bezosAge = input("Enter age: ")
3. bezosAgeModified = int(bezosAge)

E6.2. What is the purpose of the *input* function?

E6.3. What is the function name used to convert a value to type *str*?

Practical exercises

E6.4. Write a program that asks the user to input their first name, last name, age, and height. Store each value in a separate variable (you will have four variables). Finally, print the contents and type of each variable. **Note:** when requesting input from the user, convert the values to the most appropriate types.

E6.5. Write a program that asks the user to enter their first name and last name via keyboard input. The program should print the last name, followed by a space, and then the first name, all on the same line. **Hint:** to insert a space in between, concatenate the last name with " " and then concatenate the first name.

Input example	Output example
Sebastian Gomez	Gomez Sebastian

E6.6. A crazy scientist always miscalculates the years when an asteroid will likely fall to Earth. If the scientist says that an asteroid will fall in 10 years, it's because it will fall in 5 years (he always overestimates the actual number of years by double). Write a program that asks the user to enter the number of years until an asteroid falls (according to the crazy scientist, in *float* format). Then, print the text "The asteroid will fall in:", concatenate it with the actual result of the years until it falls, and finally, concatenate it with the text "years".

Input example	Output example
28.4	The asteroid will fall in: 14.2 years

Summary

In this chapter, we learned how to perform input and output operations. For input, we learned to use the *input* function to collect user input from the keyboard. Additionally, we learned to use the *int*, *str*, and *float* functions for type conversions, which are convenient when performing mathematical operations or concatenating data in output statements. For output, we learned how to use the *print* function, how to pass values or variables to it, and how to concatenate data to reduce the number of prints using the "+" operator.

 **Cheat Sheet:** Now, we will take the Cheat Sheet and mark the tricks related to the topics learned in this chapter. Mark the following tricks with an "X": T12, T13, T14, T15, and T16.

In the next chapter, we will learn how to define conditions in our programs.

Chapter 07 – Simple conditionals

The evaluation of conditions is a crucial element in the programs we use daily. For instance, when we withdraw money from an ATM, the program checks whether the amount we want to withdraw is less than or equal to the balance in our account. Similarly, when we log in to our email account, the program verifies that the login credentials we enter match the authentication data stored in the system. In video games, the program checks if our character has any lives left when it dies; if not, the game ends.

In this chapter, we will learn how to define and evaluate conditions. Additionally, we will explain how to program a simple conditional.

Next, we will cover the following sections:
1. Introduction.
2. Boolean variables.
3. Comparison operators.
4. Logical operators.
5. If-then statements.
6. Flow of execution.
7. Exercises.

The code developed for this chapter is located at https://github.com/PracticalBooks/Python-For-Beginners/tree/main/Chapter07. We recommend that you develop the code by yourself to improve your coding skills. Then, in case of any issues, you can compare your code with the code available in the repository.

Remember that we suggest you create a new Colab document for each book chapter. It will allow you to keep your codes organized.

7.1. Introduction

Let's analyze the following example to understand the importance of conditionals better. In line 1 of the following code, we ask the user to enter the length of a square's side, which we convert to a float and store in the variable *side*. Then, in line 2, we calculate the square area using the value of the *side* entered previously. Finally, in line 3, we print the result on the screen.

Code and execute

1. side = float(input("Enter the length of the square's side: "))
2. area = side*side
3. print("The area of the square is: "+str(area))

So far, the code seems well-defined. If we execute the above code and enter *8*, the program will display on the screen: *"The area of the square is: 64.0"*. However, problems arise when, for example, we execute the above code again and enter *-8*. In this case, the program will execute normally and display the same result as before: *"The area of the square is: 64.0"*. But this is incorrect, as a square cannot have a side with a negative length.

To solve this problem, **we need first to check whether the user-entered value for the side length is positive (i.e., greater than zero)** before calculating the area. If the side length is greater than zero, we can calculate the area and print the result to the screen. However, if the side length is not greater than zero, we should display an error message.

We need to learn how to use conditionals to add this functionality to our code. But before we do that, let's review some important concepts.

7.2. Boolean variables

So far, we have been working with variables and values of type *int*, *float*, and *str*. These three types of variables allow us to store a wide range of values. However, to work with conditional statements, we need to learn to use a new type of variable: Boolean variables.

A **Boolean variable (bool)** can only store *True* or *False* values. *True* is typically associated with "Yes" and *False* is associated with "No". These variables or values are usually used to evaluate conditions or comparisons (as we'll see in this chapter).

Line 1 of the following code shows the creation of a Boolean variable called *hasKids*, which we use to indicate whether a person has kids or not. Then, in line 2, we print its type, and in line 3, its value. Figure 7-1 shows the graphical representation of the *hasKids* variable.

Code and execute

1. hasKids = True
2. print(type(hasKids))
3. print(hasKids)

Figure 7-1. Graphical representation of the *hasKids* variable.

Note: Boolean variable values should not be defined with quotes (*True* or *False* should be written without quotes). If quotes are used, it would no longer define a *bool* variable but rather an *str*.

7.3. Comparison operators

Before defining conditions in Python, we must learn how to compare values. How do we compare two values? How do we know if a side is greater than zero, equal to zero, or less than zero?

In programming, **comparison operators** allow us to compare two values and evaluate the result of that comparison in a single Boolean value (*True* or *False*). Python provides six comparison operators (described in Table 7-1).

Table 7-1. Comparison operators.

Operator	Meaning
==	Equal to
!=	Not equal to
<	Less than
>	Greater than
<=	Less than or equal to
>=	Greater than or equal to

Let's practice using comparison operators with the following example. Suppose we create a variable called *side* with a value of *5*. The results of performing a series of comparisons on the *side* variable are shown in Table 7-2.

Table 7-2. Comparisons on *side = 5*.

Comparison	Result
side < 0	False
side >= 2	True
side != 5	False
side == 5	True
side > -3	True
side <= 120	True

Quick discussion: In Python, it is important to learn to differentiate the single equal sign "=" from the double equal sign "==". The "=" (assignment operator) is used to assign a value to a variable. The "==" (comparison operator) is used to compare two values.

7.4. Logical operators

Boolean values (*True* and *False*) can also be compared to each other. Like comparison operators, **logical operators** allow you to compare Boolean values and evaluate the result of those comparisons into a single Boolean value (*True* or *False*)

Logical operators are useful when we want to perform multiple comparisons together. For example, checking that a person is of legal age and, at the same time, has enough money to buy a beer.

Python provides three logical operators (see Table 7-3).

Table 7-3. Logical operators.

Operator
and
or
not

and operator

The *and* operator compares two Boolean values or expressions. This operator **evaluates to *True* if both Boolean values (or expressions) are true. Otherwise, it evaluates to *False***.

Table 7-4 shows the possible combinations and results when using the *and* operator.

Table 7-4. Truth table for the *and* operator.

Expression	Result
True *and* True	True
True *and* False	False
False *and* True	False
False *and* False	False

Let's practice using the *and* operator with the following exercise. Suppose a variable called *age* is created with a value of *18* and a variable called *name* is created with a value of *"Paola"*. Let's see in Table 7-5 the result of evaluating a series of expressions using both variables.

Table 7-5. Using the *and* operator on *age = 18* and *name = "Paola"*.

Expression	Result
(age == 18) *and* (name == "Paola")	True
(age > 20) *and* (name == "Paola")	False
(age <= 60) *and* (name != "Rosa")	True
(age != 18) *and* (name == "Paola")	False

Let's analyze step by step the second expression: *(age > 20) and (name == "Paola")*. (1) We evaluate the comparison on the left. The *age* is not greater than *20* so that comparison evaluates to *False*. (2) We evaluate the comparison on the right. The name is equal to *"Paola"*, consequently, that comparison evaluates to *True*. Finally, (3) we must evaluate: *(False) and (True)*. And as we saw in the truth table of the *and* operator, that expression evaluates to *False*. Figure 7-2 shows the step-by-step evaluation of this expression.

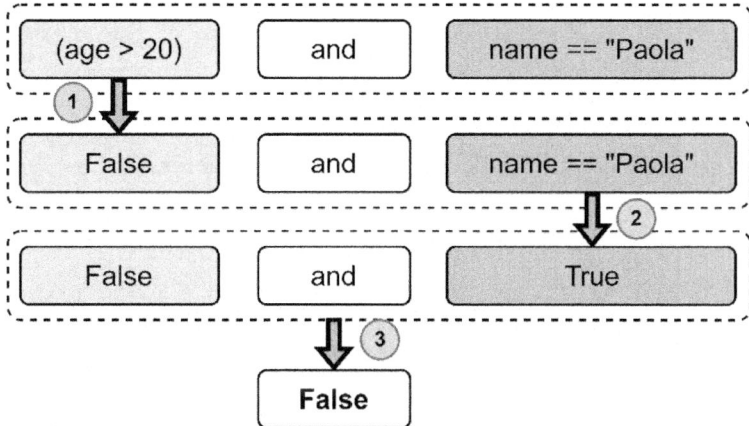

Figure 7-2. Evaluation of the expression *(age > 20) and (name == "Paola")*.

or operator

The *or* operator compares two Boolean values (or expressions). This operator **evaluates the comparison to *True* if either Boolean value (or expression) is true. Only if both are false does it evaluate to *False***.

Table 7-6 shows the possible combinations and results when using the *or* operator.

Table 7-6. Truth table for the *or* operator.

Expression	Result
True *or* True	True
True *or* False	True
False *or* True	True
False *or* False	False

Let's practice using the *or* operator with the following exercise. Suppose a variable called *age* is created with a value of *18* and a variable called *name* is created with a value of *"Paola"*. Let's see in Table 7-7 the result of evaluating a series of expressions using both variables.

Table 7-7. Using the *or* operator on *age = 18* and *name = "Paola"*.

Expression	Result
(age == 18) *or* (name == "Paola")	True
(age > 20) *or* (name == "Rosa")	False
(age <= 60) *or* (name != "Rosa")	True
(age != 18) *or* (name == "Paola")	True

not operator

The not operator (negation) operates on a single Boolean value or expression. This operator **evaluates to the opposite value of the Boolean value of the expression**.

Table 7-8 shows the possible combinations and results when using the *not* operator.

Table 7-8. Truth table for the *not* operator.

Expression	Result
not True	False
not False	True

Let's practice using the *not* operator with the following exercise. Suppose a variable called *age* is created with a value of *18*, and a variable called *hasKids* is created with a value of *True*. Let's see in Table 7-9 the result of evaluating a series of expressions using both variables.

Table 7-9. Using the *not* operator on *age = 18* and *hasKids = True*.

Expression	Result
not(hasKids)	False
not(age > 20)	True
not(age <= 60)	False
not(age == 18)	False

Now that we know how to use comparison operators and logical operators, we can start using conditionals in Python.

7.5. If-then statement

Let's start working with conditionals in Python. Conditionals, or **conditional statements**, are groups of instructions that can be executed or not depending on the value of a condition.

Several conditional statements are available, but in this chapter, we will focus on the most basic one: the *if-then* statement.

if-then statement

An *if-then* statement has a structure, as presented in Figure 7-3.

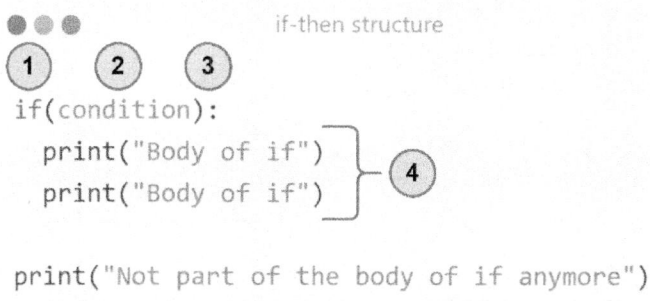

Figure 7-3. Structure of the *if-then* conditional statement.

The *if-then* statement consists of the following main elements:
1. It starts with the Python reserved word **if**.
2. A **condition or expression** is defined and must evaluate to a Boolean value. This condition or expression may or may not be enclosed in parentheses.
3. A colon ":" is used to indicate the start of the body of the *if*.

4. The **body of the *if*** statement is defined. This is where we place the instruction(s) to be executed if the previous condition or expression evaluates to *True*. These instruction(s) should be indented as code blocks, i.e., moved to the right (with respect to the location of the if statement) using a tab.

Example flowchart for *if-then* structure

Before we start coding our first conditional, let's see how to represent a scenario where conditionals are needed using a flowchart. Let's suppose we are developing a program to remind us to buy ice cream when it's hot outside. The program will receive the current temperature (in degrees Celsius) through the keyboard, and if the temperature is greater than *27*, it will print the message "Buy ice cream". Finally, the program will always print the message "End of program" before finishing.

Figure 7-4 shows the graphical representation of the previous program. In this diagram, the ***if* section** (the condition) is represented by the diamond shape. The ***then* section** is represented by the *True* path, until it meets the *False* path. In this program, the message "Buy ice cream" will only be printed (the *then* section will be executed) when the condition is met.

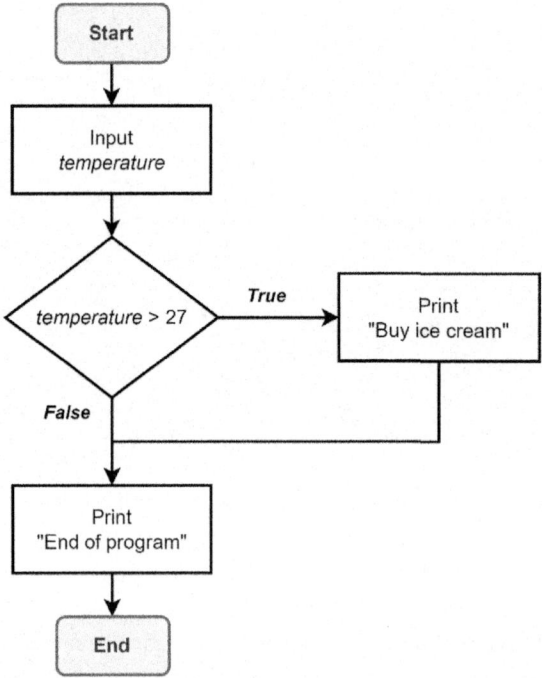

Figure 7-4. Flowchart for the "ice cream" exercise with *if-then* structure.

Example code for the *if-then* structure

The following code shows the implementation of the previous flowchart. In line 1, the user is asked to enter the current temperature. Then, in line 3, the *if* statement is executed, which evaluates if the temperature is greater than *27*. If the condition evaluates to *True*, line 4 is executed (since it corresponds to the body of the if statement), and the message *"Buy ice cream"* is printed. Finally, line 6 is executed, and the message *"End of program"* is printed.

Code and execute

```
1.  temperature = float(input("Enter the temperature: "))
2.
3.  if(temperature > 27):
4.     print("Buy ice cream")
5.
6.  print("End of program")
```

If you execute the previous code and enter the number *28*, you will get a result like the one presented in Figure 7-5.

```
Enter the temperature: 28
Buy ice cream
End of program
```
Figure 7-5. Execution of the previous code by entering *28*.

Quick discussion: What happens when executing the previous code and the number entered is not greater than 27? If you execute the previous code and enter the number 27, Python ignores (skips) the lines belonging to the body of the if statement (those indented under the if statement). In this case, line 4 is ignored. However, line 6 is executed since it is not part of the body of the if statement.

Body of the *if-then* structure

The body of an *if-then* statement is the code block immediately following the *if* statement, which is indented. Let's analyze in detail how this body works with the following example. Suppose you are asked to modify the previous code so that when the temperature is greater than 27, the message "Buy ice cream" is printed, but also the message "Buy milkshake" (see Figure 7-6).

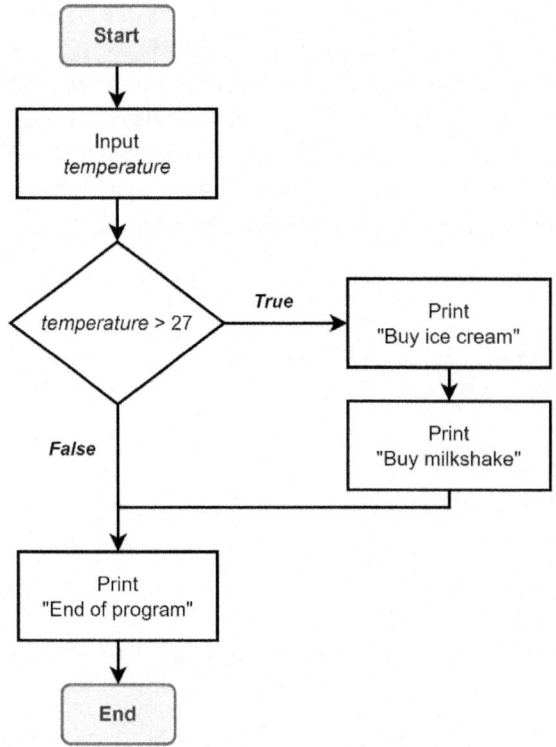

Figure 7-6. Flowchart for the "ice cream" exercise modified.

The following code shows a first attempt to solve the previous exercise. In this code, line 5 was added to print the message "Buy milkshake". However, if we run the code and enter the number 5 for the temperature, the computer will always show us the messages "Buy milkshake" and "End of program". This behavior is not desired since we could only buy a milkshake if the temperature was greater than 27.

Code and execute

1. temperature = float(input("Enter the temperature: "))
2.
3. if(temperature > 27):
4.   print("Buy ice cream")
5. **print("Buy milkshake")**
6.
7. print("End of program")

The problem is that line 5 doesn't belong to the body of the if statement because it is not indented. To fix it, we need to add a tabulation so that it becomes part of the if body (as shown in the following code). With this change, our code is now consistent with the requested exercise.

Code and execute

```
1.  temperature = float(input("Enter the temperature: "))
2.
3.  if(temperature > 27):
4.      print("Buy ice cream")
5.      print("Buy milkshake")
6.
7.  print("End of program")
```

Quick discussion: Indentation in Python plays a crucial role. It is important to pay close attention to when to indent a set of instructions and when not to, as it can completely change the logic of our program.

7.6. Flow of execution

Understanding which lines of code are executed and which are not, for a particular program is crucial if we want to develop programming logic. Before this chapter, we took for granted that all lines of our programs were executed. However, with the introduction of conditionals, we saw this was not the case.

Let's take the "ice cream" exercise again and apply a small change, and then we will show the flow of execution for this program. Now the program will receive the current temperature (in degrees Celsius) and the amount of cash we have (in dollars) through the keyboard. If the temperature is greater than 27 and the cash is greater than or equal to 5, then the program will print the message "Buy ice cream" on the screen. Finally, the program will always print the message "End of program" before finishing.

The following code shows the implementation of the previous exercise. As we can see, line 2 is added to request the amount of cash through the keyboard, and the conditional on line 4 is modified using the *and* operator and evaluating both comparisons.

Code and execute

1. temperature = float(input("Enter the temperature: "))
2. cash = float(input("Enter the amount of cash: "))
3.
4. if(temperature > 27) and (cash >= 5):
5.   print("Buy ice cream")
6.
7. print("End of program")

Execution flow for inputs *28* and *6*

Suppose we execute the previous code and enter *28* and *6*, respectively. The expression on line 4 evaluates to *True*, and therefore, line 5 is executed. If we track the lines that are executed step by step, we find that the following lines are executed: 1, 2, 4, 5, and 7 (see step-by-step execution in Figure 7-7). **Note:** remember that the numbers in a black background circle indicate the step-by-step execution of the program. In this case, step 1 executes line 1, step 2 executes line 2, step 3 executes line 4, step 4 executes line 5, and step 5 executes line 7.

```
1 ❶ temperature = float(input("Enter the temperature: "))
2 ❷ cash = float(input("Enter the amount of cash: "))
3
4 ❸ if(temperature > 27) and (cash >= 5):
5 ❹     print("Buy ice cream")
6
7 ❺ print("End of program")
```

Figure 7-7. Step-by-step execution flow of the previous code by entering *28* and *6*, respectively.

Execution flow for inputs *28* and *4*

Now, if we execute the previous code again and enter *28* and *4*, respectively, the expression in line 4 will evaluate to *False*, and therefore line 5 will not be executed. If we track the lines executed step by step, we find that lines 1, 2, 4, and 7 are executed (see step-by-step execution in Figure 7-8).

```
1 ❶ temperature = float(input("Enter the temperature: "))
2 ❷ cash = float(input("Enter the amount of cash: "))
3
4 ❸ if(temperature > 27) and (cash >= 5):
5      print("Buy ice cream")
6
7 ❹ print("End of program")
```

Figure 7-8. Step-by-step execution flow of the previous code by entering *28* and *4*, respectively.

7.7. Exercises

Theoretical exercises

E7.1. Analyze the following code and mention which lines of code are executed.

Analyze

1. tickets = 5
2. if(tickets > 5):
3.   print("You and your friends can enter")
4. print("End of program")

E7.2. What is the purpose of the *and* operator, and when does it evaluate to *True*?

E7.3. Considering the variable *load = 200* and the variable type = "Tractor", indicate whether each of the following expressions evaluates to *True* or *False*.

Expression	Result
(load == 200) *and* (type != "Truck")	?
(load > 350) *or* (type == "Tractor")	?
(load <= 600) *and* (type != "Tractor")	?
not(type == "Truck")	?

Practical exercises

E7.4. Write a program that asks the user to enter the distance in miles at which their partner is located (who is home alone). If the entered distance is less than or equal to 4, print "I'm coming over".

E7.5. Write a program that asks the user to enter by keyboard the jersey number of a soccer player. If the number is equal to *19*, print *"What are you looking at fool? Get back there"*.

E7.6. A tsunami monitoring station needs a system to issue alerts. The station must issue an alert when an earthquake of magnitude 5.2 or greater occurs. Implement a program that asks the user to enter the magnitude of an earthquake by the keyboard. If the entered magnitude is greater than or equal to 5.2, print *"Tsunami alert!!"*.

Input example	Output example
5.4	*Tsunami alert!!*

Summary

In this chapter, we learned the basics of using conditionals in Python and programming in general. We learned about a new type of variable (*bool*). We learned how to use six types of comparison operators (>, >=, <, <=, ==, and *!=*). We learned about the three types of logical operators (*and*, *or*, and *not*). Finally, we learned about the *if-then* statement and how the program's flow of execution varies depending on how expressions or conditions in our programs are evaluated, and how the lines below the conditional are indented (tabulated).

 **Cheat Sheet:** Now, we will take the Cheat Sheet and mark the tricks related to the topics learned in this chapter. Mark the following tricks with an "X": T04, T17, T18, T19, T20, T21, T22, T23, T24, T25, T26, and T27.

In the next chapter, we will learn about other types of conditional structures.

Chapter 08 – Multiple conditionals

In the previous chapter, we learned the basics of conditionals in Python. In this chapter, we will cover additional conditional structures and work on more complex scenarios.

Next, we will cover the following sections:
1. The *if-then-else* statement.
2. The *if-then-elif-else* statement.
3. Nested conditionals.
4. Exercises.

The code developed for this chapter is located at https://github.com/PracticalBooks/Python-For-Beginners/tree/main/Chapter08. We recommend that you develop the code by yourself to improve your coding skills. Then, in case of any issues, you can compare your code with the code available in the repository.

Remember that we suggest you create a new Colab document for each book chapter. It will allow you to keep your codes organized.

8.1. The if-then-else statement

In the previous chapter, we covered the *if-then* statement, which allowed us to execute a series of instructions if a condition evaluated to *True*. However, it's common to want to execute instructions when the condition is not met (i.e., evaluates to *False*). For example, if a condition is met (i.e., the square's side is greater than zero), we can calculate the square's area. Otherwise, if the condition is not met (i.e., the square's side is negative or zero), we can print an error message.

In Python, the *if-then* statement can be expanded using an *else* section, which generates an *if-then-else* statement. The **if-then-else** statement can be read as follows: **If** this condition is true, **then** execute the following instructions. Otherwise (**else**), execute these other instructions.

if-then-else **structure**

Since we have previously explained the *if-then* structure, here we will only detail the new *else* section, which has a structure as shown in Figure 8-1.

```
if(condition):
    print("Body of if")
 ①  print("Body of if")
    else: ②
        print("Body of else")
        print("Body of else")   ③
```

Figure 8-1. *else* section of the *if-then-else* structure.

1. The Python reserved word ***else*** is used (it should be placed right after the *then* section of the conditional and must maintain the same indentation level as the *if* statement that contains it).
2. A colon "**:**" is used to indicate the start of the body of *else*.
3. The **body of *else*** is defined. This is where we place the instruction(s) that would be executed if the condition or expression evaluates to *False*. This instruction(s) should be indented as code blocks, i.e., moved from left to right (with respect to the location of the *else* section) using a tab.

Example flowchart for *if-then-else* structure

Let's take the example of the "ice cream" program but with some modifications. The program will receive the current temperature (in degrees Celsius) via keyboard, and if the temperature is higher than 27, it will print the message "Buy ice cream". Otherwise, the program will print the message "Buy orange juice". Finally, the program will always print the message "End of program" before ending.

Figure 8-2 shows the graphical representation of the previous program. In this diagram, the ***if* section** (the condition) is represented by the diamond. The ***then* section** is represented by the *True* path. And the ***else* section** is represented by the *False* path. In this program, only when the condition is not met, the message *"Buy orange juice"* will be printed (the *else* section will be executed).

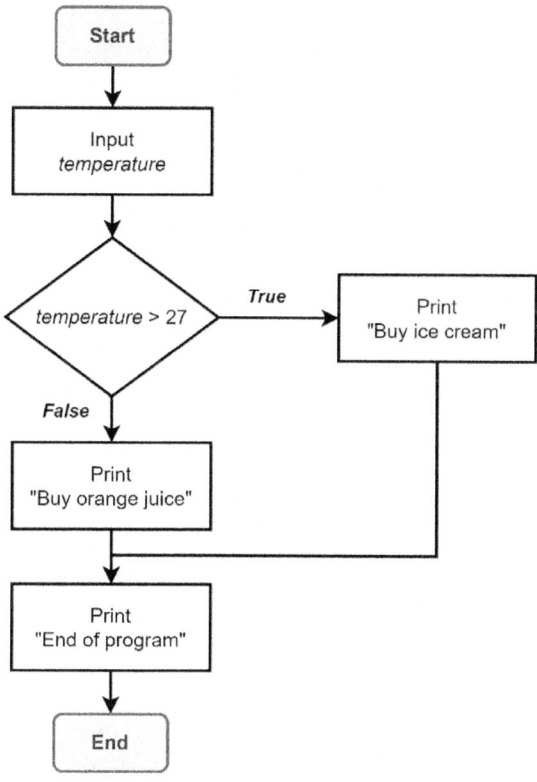

Figure 8-2. Flowchart for the "ice cream" exercise with *if-then-else* structure.

Example code for the *if-then-else* structure

The following code shows the implementation of the previous flowchart. Since we have already explained part of this code, let's carefully analyze the new elements. In line 5, the *else* section is added, and in line 6, the body of the *else* is added (the instruction that will be executed when the condition evaluates to *False*).

Code and execute

```
1.  temperature = float(input("Enter the temperature: "))
2.
3.  if(temperature > 27):
4.     print("Buy ice cream")
5.  else:
6.     print("Buy orange juice")
7.
8.  print("End of program")
```

If you execute the previous code and enter the number *22*, you will get a result like the one presented in Figure 8-3. This is because the program will initially execute line 1 (and assign the number *22* to the variable *temperature*), then execute line 3 (the condition evaluates to *False* since *22* is not greater than *27*). Then, the program will jump to line 5 (to the *else* section), execute line 6, and finally execute line 8.

```
Enter the temperature: 22
Buy orange juice
End of program
```

Figure 8-3. Execution of the previous code by entering *22*.

Exercise: Area of a Square

Now that we have the necessary tools, we can solve the exercise we introduced when discussing conditionals. This exercise required calculating the area of a square when a side with a value greater than zero was entered and printing an error message for any other value.

The following code shows the solution to that exercise. But before running it, let's try to answer the following questions: (i) if the following code is executed and the number 3 is entered via keyboard, which lines will be executed? And how many variables would be created in memory? And (ii) if the following program is executed and the number -3 is entered via keyboard, which lines will be executed? And how many variables would be created in memory?

Code and execute

1. side = float(input("Enter the length of the square's side: "))
2.
3. if(side > 0):
4.   area = side*side
5.   print("The area of the square is: "+str(area))
6. else:
7.   print("Square's side must be greater than zero")

Answer for the input value of 3: (i) Lines 1, 3, 4, and 5 would be executed. (ii) Two variables (*side* and *area*) would be created in memory.

Answer for the input value of -3: (i) Lines 1, 3, 6, and 7 would be executed. (ii) One variable (*side*) would be created in memory.

8.2. The if-then-elif-else statement

Regardless of its structure, a conditional can have at most one *if* section and one *else* section (which goes at the end). However, a conditional can optionally be extended using one or more *elif* sections.

An *elif* section can only be placed right after the *if* section or after another *elif* section.

The **elif section** (the abbreviated version of "else if") allows for defining an additional condition that is evaluated only if all previous conditions were false. It also defines in its body a set of instructions that will be executed if the *elif* condition evaluates to *True*.

For example, let's suppose we want to verify a person's age to assign them to a Covid-19 vaccination stage. In this case, a simple *if-then-else* statement will not be enough since we have multiple vaccination stages and age verifications to consider. In the current scenario, we could check **if** the age is greater than or equal to 70 years old and assign that person to stage 1 of vaccination. **Otherwise, if** the age is greater than or equal to 60 years old and less than 70 years old, assign that person to stage 2 of vaccination. **Otherwise, if** the age is greater than or equal to 30 years old and less than 60 years old, assign that person to stage 3 of vaccination. And **otherwise**, assign that person to stage 4 of vaccination.

if-then-elif-else structure

Since we have previously explained the *if-then-else* structure, here we will only detail the new *elif* section, which has a structure as shown in Figure 8-4.

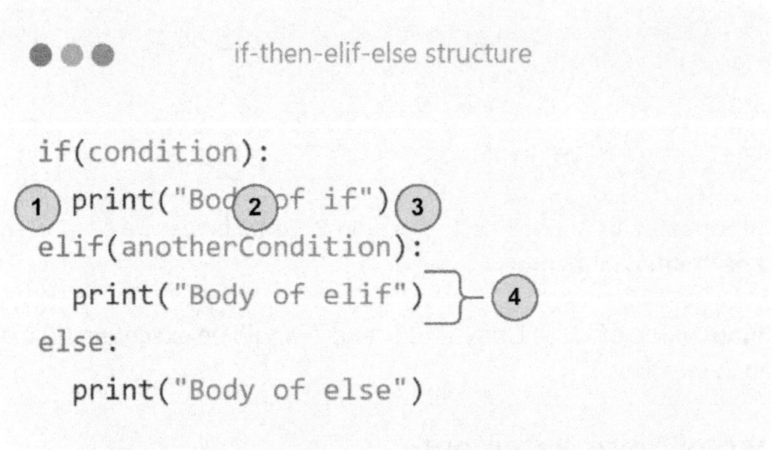

```
if(condition):
    print("Body of if")
elif(anotherCondition):
    print("Body of elif")
else:
    print("Body of else")
```

if-then-elif-else structure

Figure 8-4. *elif* section of the *if-then-elif-else* structure.

1. The Python reserved word **elif** is used (it should be placed after an *if* or another *elif*).
2. A new **condition or expression** is defined that must evaluate to a Boolean value. This condition will only be evaluated if all previous conditions were evaluated as *False*.
3. A colon ":" is used to indicate the start of the body of *elif*.
4. The **body of elif** is defined. This is where we place the instruction(s) that would be executed if the *elif* condition evaluates to *True*. This instruction(s) should be placed as indented code blocks, i.e., moved from left to right (with respect to the location of the *elif* section) using a tab.

Example flowchart for *if-then-elif-else* structure

Let's take the example of the "ice cream" program but with some modifications. The program will receive the current temperature (in degrees Celsius) via keyboard, and if the temperature is greater than 27, then it will print the message "Buy ice cream". Otherwise, if the temperature is less than 15, then it will print the message "Buy chocolate". Otherwise, the program will print the message "Buy orange juice". Finally, the program will always print the message "End of program" before ending.

Figure 8-5 shows the graphical representation of the previous program. In this diagram, the *if* **section** (the condition) is represented by the first diamond. The *then* **section** is represented by the

True path of the first diamond. The ***elif* section** (the other condition) is represented by the second diamond (which connects to the *False* path of the first diamond). And the ***else* section** is represented by the *False* path of the second diamond. In this program, only when the first condition is not met and the second condition is met, the message "Buy chocolate" will be printed (the *elif* section will be executed).

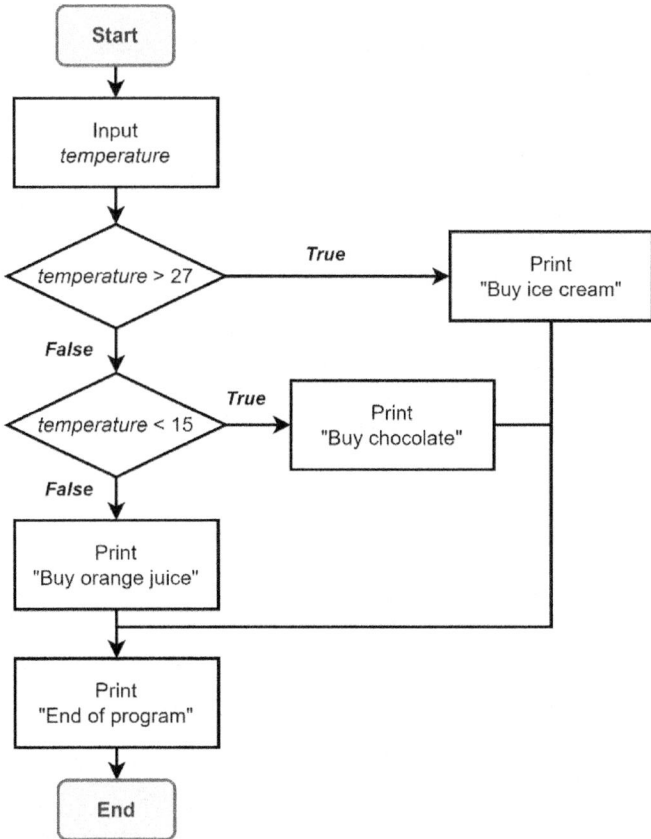

Figure 8-5. Flowchart for the "ice cream" exercise with *if-then-elif-else* structure.

Example code for the *if-then-elif-else* structure

The following code shows the implementation of the previous flowchart. Since we have already explained part of this code, let's carefully analyze the new elements. On line 5, the *elif* section is added, and a new condition is added to this section to check if the *temperature* is less than *15*. And on line 6, the body of *elif* is added (the instruction that will be executed when the condition of the *elif* evaluates to *True*). Remember that the *elif* will only be executed if the previous conditions (in this case, the previous if statement) evaluated to *False*.

Code and execute

```
1.   temperature = float(input("Enter the temperature: "))
2.
3.   if(temperature > 27):
4.       print("Buy ice cream")
5.   elif(temperature < 15):
6.       print("Buy chocolate")
7.   else:
8.       print("Buy orange juice")
9.
10.  print("End of program")
```

If you execute the previous code and enter the number 7, you should get a result like the one presented in Figure 8-6. The program will initially execute line 1 (and assign the number *7* to the variable *temperature*), then execute line 3 (here, the comparison would evaluate to *False*, since *7* is not greater than *27*). Then the program will jump to line 5 (to the *elif* section), in this case, the comparison would evaluate to *True*. Therefore, it will execute line 6. Finally, it will skip the *else* section and execute line 10.

```
Enter the temperature: 7
Buy chocolate
End of program
```

Figure 8-6. Execution of the previous code by entering 7.

The importance of condition ordering

Let's analyze the following code to answer the question: What value of age would print the message "Older adult"?

Code and execute

1. age = int(input("Enter you age: "))
2.
3. if(age >= 18):
4.   print("Adult")
5. elif(age >= 65):
6.   print("Older adult")

Answer: None. Because the first condition encompasses the values of the second condition. For example, if we input *68*, the code would first evaluate the *if* statement on line 3, and since 68 is greater than or equal to 18, it would print *"Adult"* (and skip the *elif* statement). For this exercise, the conditions should have been defined in the opposite order (first checking *age* greater than or equal to *65*, and then checking *age* greater than or equal to *18*).

Note: The order in which conditions are defined is important when using *elif* statements.

8.3. Nested conditionals

In programming, it's common to have conditions inside other conditions, called **nested conditionals**. Sometimes, we need to check an initial condition first, and if that condition is met, then we perform a series of actions that may include new conditions.

For example, let's say we're creating an access system for a theme park's attractions. First, the program will ask the user to enter the type of attraction they want to access (there are only two options: 1 for roller coaster and 2 for train ride).
- If the user **enters 1**: (i) the program will ask the user to input their height. (ii) If the height is greater than or equal to 121.92 (let's assume that's the minimum height to ride the roller coaster), it will print *"Enjoy the roller coaster"*. And (iii) otherwise, it will print *"Height not allowed"*.
- Otherwise, if the user **enters 2**, it will print *"Enjoy the train ride"*.

Finally, in the end, the program will always print the message *"End of program"*.

Next, let's see the graphical representation of the previous exercise and its code solution.

Example diagram for "amusement park" exercise

Figure 8-7 shows the graphical representation of the previous program. In this diagram, we see the nested conditional contained in the box with dotted lines. If the user enters *attractionType* as *1*, then they will be prompted to enter their *height*, and finally, the second conditional (nested conditional) will be executed.

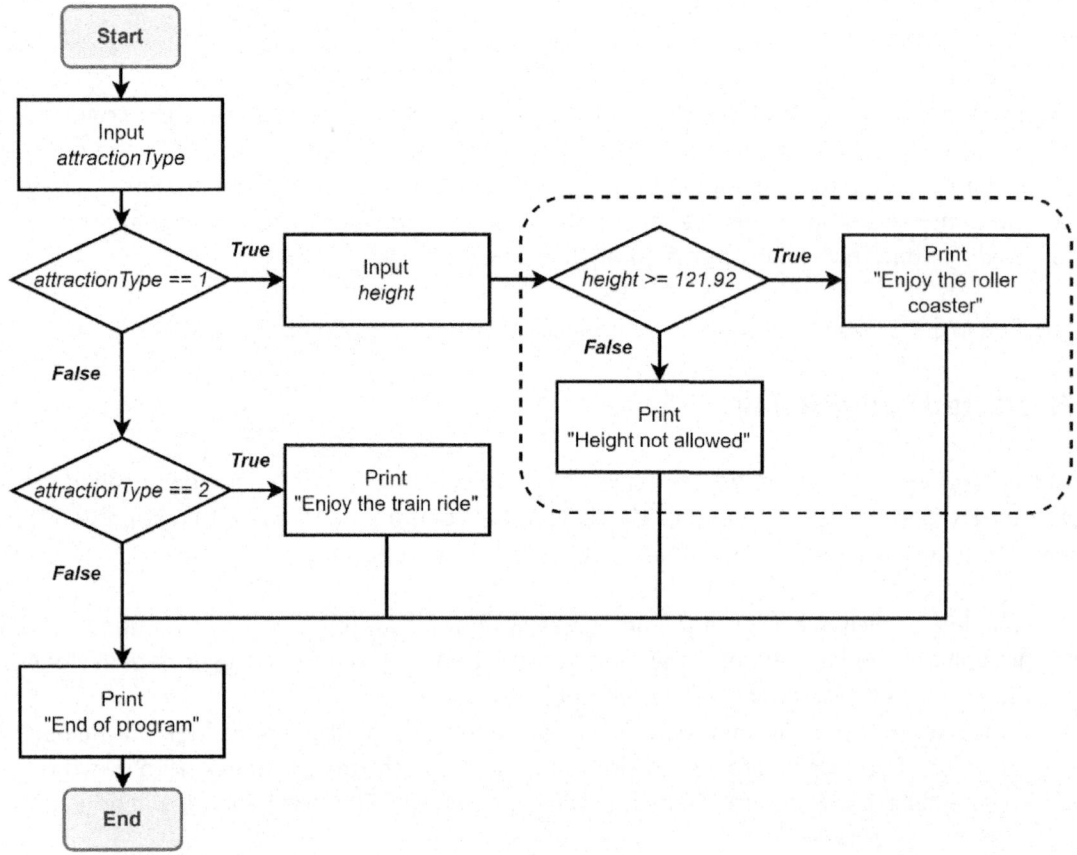

Figure 8-7. Flowchart of the "amusement park" exercise with nested conditional.

Example code for "amusement park" exercise

The following code shows the implementation of the previous flowchart. In this case, we will focus on explaining the nested conditional. In line 3, it is checked if the user entered *attractionType* equal to *1*, which means they want to ride the roller coaster. Only for this case, an additional verification must be performed. In line 4, the user is prompted to enter their *height*. Then, in line 5, it is checked if the entered *height* is greater than or equal to *121.92*. **Here we have the nested**

conditional. Since it is a conditional statement contained within the body of another conditional, the nested *if* and *else* statements must be indented twice.

Code and execute

```
1.  attractionType = int(input("Enter type 1) roller coaster 2) train: "))
2.
3.  if(attractionType == 1):
4.    height = float(input("Enter your height: "))
5.    if(height >= 121.92):
6.      print("Enjoy the roller coaster")
7.    else:
8.      print("Height not allowed")
9.  elif(attractionType == 2):
10.   print("Enjoy the train ride")
11.
12. print("End of program")
```

If you execute the previous program and enter *1* and *160.62*, respectively, you should get a result like the one presented in Figure 8-8.

```
Enter type 1) roller coaster 2) train: 1
Enter your height: 160.62
Enjoy the roller coaster
End of program
```
Figure 8-8. Execution of the previous code by entering *1* and *160.62*, respectively.

Quick discussion: In programming, there are different strategies for solving the same problem. We could have solved the previous exercise without nested conditionals (as shown in the following code). The problem with the following code is that the user experience could be better. Regardless of the type of attraction selected, the program always asks for height (in real life, if I am going to board a train ride, I shouldn't have to give my height). That's why the previous solution (with nested conditionals) seems to fit better for this particular problem.

Code and execute

```
1.  attractionType = int(input("Enter type 1) roller coaster 2) train: "))
2.  height = float(input("Enter your height: "))
3.
4.  if(attractionType == 2):
5.     print("Enjoy the train ride")
6.  elif(attractionType == 1 and height >= 121.92):
7.     print("Enjoy the roller coaster")
8.  elif(attractionType == 1 and height < 121.92):
9.     print("Height not allowed")
10.
11. print("End of program")
```

8.4. Exercises

Theoretical exercises

E8.1. Analyze the following code and mention which lines of code are executed.

Analyze

```
1.  stars = 2
2.  if(stars > 3):
3.     print("Would recommend")
4.  else:
5.     print("Would not recommend")
6.  print("End of program")
```

E8.2. True or false. Does an *elif* section only get evaluated if all previous conditions evaluated to false?

E8.3. Analyze the following code and say what it prints.

Analyze

1. amountOfSpilledPaint = 20
2. if(amountOfSpilledPaint >= 15):
3.   print("Flappin flotsam, what's that")
4. elif(amountOfSpilledPaint > 0):
5.   print("You could do better")
6. else:
7.   print("You rock!")
8. print("End of program")

Practical exercises

E8.4. Write a program that asks the user to input their favorite musical genre via keyboard. If the genre is *"Rock"*, print *"You have good taste"*. Otherwise, print *"Disgusting"*.

E8.5. Your daughter's school needs you to help design a program to determine who won the class representative elections. There are two student candidates, and the one with the highest vote count wins. Implement a program that asks the user to input the following via keyboard: the name of the first student, the vote count of the first student, the name of the second student, and the vote count of the second student. The program should print to the screen the name of the winning student (if there is a tie, it should print the message *"Tie"*).

Input example	Output example
Michelle	Ronald
40	
Ronald	
50	

Summary

In this chapter, we learned new conditional structures. We learned how to use the *if-then-else, if-then-elif-else,* and nested conditionals. We learned that the *elif* section is added to a conditional when we want to perform multiple checks (adding new conditions). We learned that the *else* section is added when we want to execute instructions when the previous conditions were not met. And we learned that, in some cases, it's useful to contain conditions and instructions within other conditions.

 **Cheat Sheet:** Now, we will take the Cheat Sheet and mark the tricks related to the topics learned in this chapter. Mark the following tricks with an "X": T28, T29, and T30.

In the next chapter, we will learn the basics of loops in programming using the *while* loop in Python.

Chapter 09 – While loop

Loops are a fundamental element in programming. They allow you to execute a series of instructions multiple times, saving time and lines of code. Python offers two types of loops: *while* and *for*. In this chapter, we will explain how loops work, focusing specifically on the *while* loop. We will cover the *for* loop in a later chapter, as it's easier to understand after exploring variable types such as strings, lists, and dictionaries in more detail.

Next, we will cover the following sections:
1. Introduction.
2. Parts of loops.
3. Basic structure of a while loop.
4. Example of a while loop with step-by-step tracking.
5. Other examples and common errors.
6. Sentinel-controlled loops.
7. Break statement.
8. Exercises.

The code developed for this chapter is located at https://github.com/PracticalBooks/Python-For-Beginners/tree/main/Chapter09. We recommend that you develop the code by yourself to improve your coding skills. Then, in case of any issues, you can compare your code with the code available in the repository.

Remember that we suggest you create a new Colab document for each book chapter. It will allow you to keep your codes organized.

9.1. Introduction

The repetition of instructions is a common part of our daily programs. For example, a company may have a program that collects each worker's salary to calculate the total payroll to be paid at the end of the month. Suppose the company has 40 workers. With what we've seen so far, it would be necessary to request 40 salaries via keyboard input and then add them up and print the sum on the screen. Each salary request would require one line of code, leading to a program with a minimum of 41 lines of code. Fortunately, Python and other programming languages offer loop structures that allow a set of instructions to be repeated multiple times.

Before starting with exercises like the one above, let's see how loops work with simpler cases.

Suppose we are asked to print the message *"Welcome to Python"* 3 times on the screen. If we wanted to solve this exercise with what has been seen so far, we should implement code like the one presented below.

Code and execute

1. print("Welcome to Python")
2. print("Welcome to Python")
3. print("Welcome to Python")

Now, let's suppose we are asked to print *"Welcome to Python"* 100 times. We would have to repeat the instruction *print("Welcome to Python")* 100 times. This would imply coding 100 lines of code. But if we do it with a loop, we can code the same program with a few lines of code.

A **loop** allows grouping an instruction or a set of instructions that will be executed repeatedly (while a condition is met). That is, using a loop we can tell the computer to display a text on the screen 100 times without having to code the *print* instruction 100 times (it will be enough to code it only once).

Let's see the following example (which we will explain later):

Code and execute

1. i = 1
2. while(i <= 3):
3.   print("Welcome to Python")
4.   i = i+1
5.
6. print("End of program")

Note: if we change the number *3*, which appears in the condition of line 2, to the number *100*, and execute the program, the message *"Welcome to Python"* will appear on the screen 100 times.

9.2. Parts of loops

In general, loops are composed of four parts.

1. Initialization of the control variable: A variable is initialized to control the execution of the loop. This variable is typically assigned an initial value before the loop begins.

2. Test on the control variable: A test is performed on the control variable to verify whether the loop can or cannot continue executing.
3. Body of loop: It defines the instruction or set of instructions that would be executed repetitively while the test on the control variable evaluates to *True*.
4. Update on the control variable: Generally, before ending the body of the loop, a change is made to the control variable. This will allow the loop to stop at some point. This typically involves adding or subtracting a value from the control variable.

The flowchart on the left-hand side of Figure 9-1 shows the graphical representation of a loop with its four parts. On the right-hand side of the figure, the example of printing the message *"Welcome to Python"* three times is developed. We will analyze that diagram step by step. Likewise, throughout the book, we will practice using loops with multiple exercises.

Let's analyze step by step the right-hand side of Figure 9-1:
1. The program starts with the **initialization of the control variable** called *i*. It is commonly called "i" because it is often used as an "index" to access elements of a list (we will discuss indexes and lists in detail in the next two chapters). This control variable is given an initial value of *1*. For this exercise, *i* will help us keep track of how many times the loop is executed. If we want to print a message 3 times, we start at *1.*
2. Then a **test is performed on the control variable**. In this case, we will check that *i* does not exceed *3* (always less than or equal to *3*). Why *3*? Because it is the number of times we want to print the message.
3. The test evaluates to *True* (since *1* is less than or equal to *3*).
4. The **body of loop** is executed. Now *"Welcome to Python"* is printed (we have one print so far).
5. Then, the **control variable *i* is updated** by increasing its value by *1* (now it is *2*).
6. The program flow continues and takes us back to the **test on the control variable**.
7. The test evaluates to *True* (since *2* is less than or equal to *3*).
8. The **body of loop** is executed. Now *"Welcome to Python"* is printed (we have two prints so far).
9. Then, the **control variable *i* is updated** by increasing its value by *1* (now it is *3*).
10. The program flow continues and takes us back to the **test on the control variable**.
11. The test evaluates to *True* (since *3* is less than or equal to *3*).
12. The **body of loop** is executed. Now *"Welcome to Python"* is printed (we have three prints so far).
13. Then, the **control variable *i* is updated** by increasing its value by *1* (now it is *4*).
14. The program flow continues and takes us back to the **test on the control variable**.
15. The test evaluates to *False* (since *4* is not less than or equal to *3*).
16. The loop is exited (the *False* path is executed), and we print *"End of program"*.

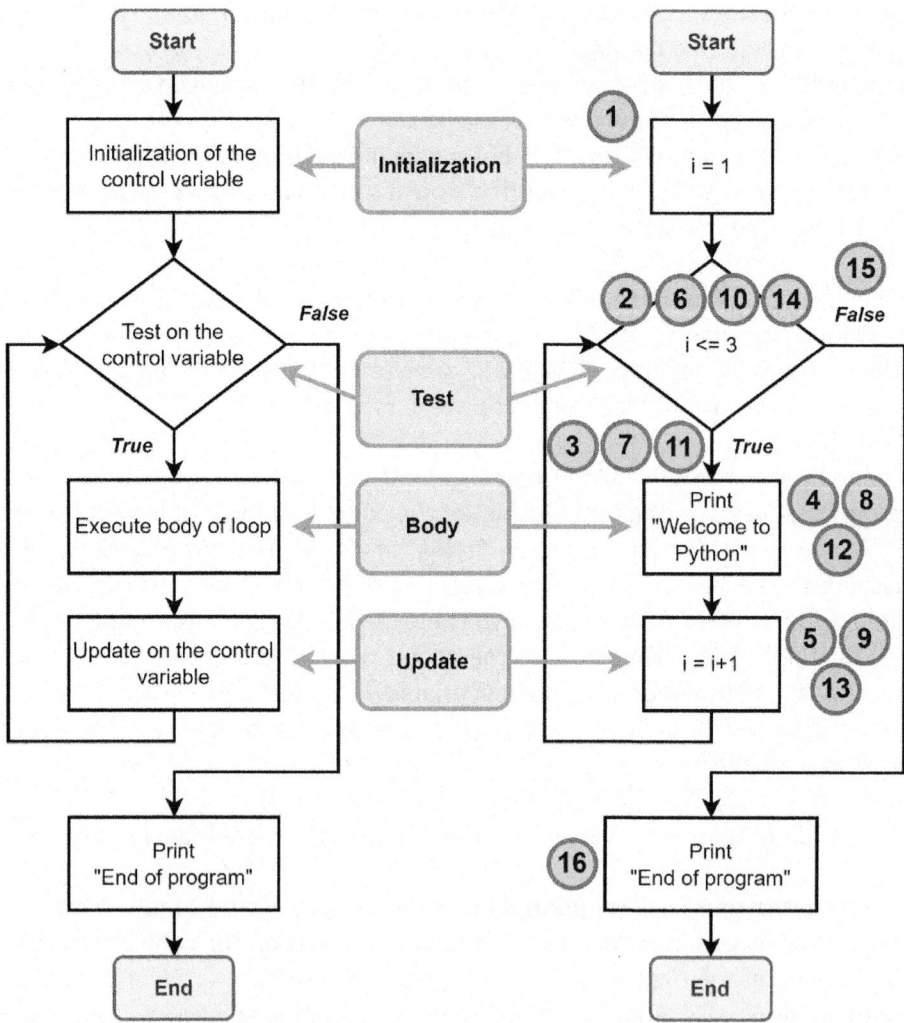

Figure 9-1. Flowchart for the representation of a loop.

Now that we have covered these general concepts about loops, let's see how the *while* loop works in Python.

9.3. Basic structure of a while loop

A ***while*** **loop** in Python executes instructions repeatedly if a condition defined within the loop is *True*. A basic *while* loop has a structure, as shown in Figure 9-2.

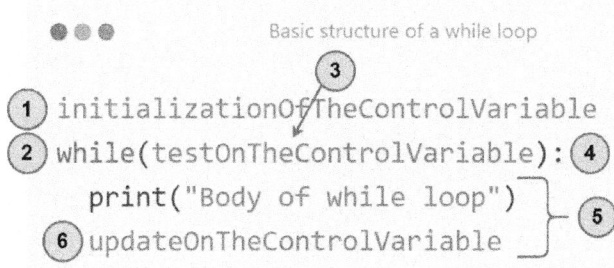

Figure 9-2. Basic structure of a *while* loop.

1. The control variable is **initialized** or defined with an initial value.
2. In the next line, the Python reserved keyword **while** is used to start defining the loop.
3. A **test** of the control variable is defined, which can be enclosed in parentheses (they are optional).
4. A colon ":" is used to indicate the start of the body of *while* loop.
5. The **body of *while* loop** is defined. This is where we place the instruction(s) to be executed if the previous condition or expression evaluates to *True*. These instruction(s) should be indented as code blocks, moving from left to right (relative to the *while* loop) with a tab.
6. Before the body of *while* loop ends, an **update** is made to the control variable.

9.4. Example of a while loop with step-by-step tracking

Let's suppose we want to print numbers from 1 to 5. We could use the code for *printing "Welcome to Python"* three times, modify the test on the control variable (now *i* will be less than or equal to 5), and modify the print line to print the value contained in our control variable. Below is the developed code.

Code and execute

1. i = 1
2. while(i <= 5):
3.   print(i)
4.   i = i+1
5.
6. print("End of program")

If you execute the previous program, you should get a result like the one shown in Figure 9-3.

```
1
2
3
4
5
End of program
```
Figure 9-3. Execution of the previous code.

Execution flow

Let's track, step by step, the previous code, paying attention to the lines that are executed and in what order they are executed (see Figure 9-4):
- **Step 1:** Line 1 is executed (which initializes the control variable *i* with a value of *1*).
- **Steps 2, 3, and 4:** Then, the first iteration of the loop is performed (the condition evaluates to *True* since *1* is less than or equal to *5*), and lines 2, 3, and 4 are executed (now *i* has a value of *2*).
- **Steps 5, 6, and 7:** Then, the second iteration of the loop is performed (the condition evaluates to *True* since *2* is less than or equal to *5*), and lines 2, 3, and 4 are executed (now *i* has a value of *3*).
- **Steps 8, 9, and 10:** Then, the third iteration of the loop is performed (the condition evaluates to *True* since *3* is less than or equal to *5*), and lines 2, 3, and 4 are executed (now *i* has a value of *4*).
- **Steps 11, 12, and 13:** Then, the fourth iteration of the loop is performed (the condition evaluates to *True* since *4* is less than or equal to *5*), and lines 2, 3, and 4 are executed (now *i* has a value of *5*).
- **Steps 14, 15, and 16:** Then, the fifth iteration of the loop is performed (the condition evaluates to *True* since *5* is less than or equal to *5*), and lines 2, 3, and 4 are executed (now *i* has a value of *6*).
- **Step 17:** At the beginning of the sixth iteration, the condition evaluates to *False* since *6* is not less than or equal to *5*. In this case, the loop is exited.
- **Step 18:** Line 6 is executed, and *"End of program"* is printed.

```
1  ①                        i = 1
2  ② ⑤ ⑧ ⑪ ⑭ ⑰  while(i <= 5):
3  ③ ⑥ ⑨ ⑫ ⑮          print(i)
4  ④ ⑦ ⑩ ⑬ ⑯          i = i+1
5
6  ⑱                        print("End of program")
```

Figure 9-4. Step-by-step execution flow of the previous code.

 **TIP:** PythonTutor (https://pythontutor.com/visualize.html) is a great tool to help you understand the step-by-step execution of your programs (just like what we did earlier). It allows you to visualize how your code is being executed and track the values of your variables as they change. You can copy and paste the code developed in Colab and then click on "Visualize Execution" and start tracking which lines are being executed step-by-step. If it's your first-time programming loops, we recommend using that tool (or a similar one) with the codes you need to analyze in detail.

9.5. Other examples and common errors

Now, we will practice implementing loops with three exercises, and then we will see a few common mistakes when programming loops.

Exercises

Exercise 1: Suppose we are asked to print the multiples of 5, from 5 to 25. The following code shows the solution to that exercise. As we can see on line 1, the control variable is initialized with a value of 5 (since we want to start printing from the number 5). On line 2, the test on the control variable is defined as *i* less than or equal to 25 (since we want to go up to the number 25). On line 3, we print the current value of *i*. And on line 4, the update on the control variable is defined as an increase of 5 units (since we want to print multiples of 5).

Code and execute

1. i = 5
2. while(i <= 25):
3.   print(i)
4.   i = i+5

Exercise 2: Suppose we are asked to print the numbers from 10 to 0 (decreasing by 1 each time). The following code shows the solution to this exercise. As we can see on line 1, the control variable is initialized with a value of *10* (since we want to start printing from the number *10*). On line 2, the condition for the control variable is set to *i* being greater than or equal to *0* (since we want to print down to the number *0* and *i* starts with a number greater than *0*). On line 3, we print the current value of *i*. And on line 4, the control variable is decremented by *1* unit.

Code and execute

1. i = 10
2. while(i >= 0):
3.   print(i)
4.   i = i-1

Exercise 3: Suppose we are asked to print the message *"Python is fun"* as many times as a number entered by the user through the keyboard. The following code shows the solution to this exercise. As we can see on line 1, we ask the user to input the number of times they want to print the message and assign that value to the variable *numberOfTimes*. Then, on line 2, the control variable is initialized with a value of *1*. Then, on line 3, the condition for the control variable is set to *i* being less than or equal to *numberOfTimes* (since we want to print up to the number entered by the user). Next, on line 4, we print the message *"Python is fun"*. And on line 5, the control variable is incremented by *1* unit. **Note:** execute the code several times, entering different numbers, and observe what happens.

Code and execute

1. numberOfTimes = int(input("Enter a number: "))
2. i = 1
3. while(i <= numberOfTimes):
4.   print("Python is fun")
5.   i = i+1

Common errors

Error 1: Analyze the following code and identify where the error is.

Analyze

1. i = 1
2. while(i <= 5):
3.   print(i)

Answer to error 1: The previous code is **missing the update on the control variable**. If the code is executed, it will print the number 1 infinitely since the condition for the control variable will never be *False*.

Error 2: Analyze the following code and identify where the error is.

Analyze

1. i = 1
2. while(i <= 5):
3.   print(i)
4. i = i+1

Answer to error 2: In the previous code, the **update to the control variable is indented incorrectly**. If the code is executed as is, it will print the number 1 infinitely since the control variable will never change its value, as the update is placed outside the body of *while* loop.

Error 3: Analyze the following code and identify where the error is.

Analyze

1. i = 1
2. while(i >= 0):
3.   print(i)
4.   i = i+1

Answer to error 3: In the previous code, the **test on the control variable is defined incorrectly**. If the code is executed as is, it will print numbers starting from *1* incrementally indefinitely. This is because the condition checks if *i* is greater than or equal to *0*, and *i* will always be greater than or equal to *0* since it starts at *1* and the update increases its value.

9.6. Sentinel-controlled loops

So far, the loops we have done have been based on tests to control numeric variables that do not depend on a special value. We know in advance how many times each loop will be executed (with a simple mathematical calculation or by counting how the control variable updates).

However, sometimes we want to control loops based on particular values that users enter as keyboard inputs. For example, creating a loop that runs until the user enters the text *"exit"*.

These types of cycles are known as **sentinel-controlled loops**. In this case, the loop will only stop when a particular value (sentinel) is entered.

The following code shows the definition of a sentinel-controlled loop. The purpose is to only welcome a user whose name is *"Daniel"*. In line 1, the control variable *name* is initialized as an empty string. Then, in line 2, it checks if the *name* is different from *"Daniel"*. If so, line 3 (the body of *while* loop) is executed, where the user is asked to enter a name on the screen. That value is assigned to the *name* variable (the update on the control variable depends on the user entering a value from the keyboard). If the user enters something different from *"Daniel"*, the loop will continue executing indefinitely. Finally, when the loop breaks (the user enters *"Daniel"*), line 5 prints the message *"Welcome"*.

Code and execute

```
1.  name = ""
2.  while(name != "Daniel"):
3.      name = input("Enter a name: ")
4.
5.  print("Welcome")
```

If you execute the previous program and enter *"Sara"* on the keyboard, then *"Juliana"*, and then *"Daniel"*, you should get a result like the one presented in Figure 9-5.

```
Enter a name: Sara
Enter a name: Juliana
Enter a name: Daniel
Welcome
```

Figure 9-5. Execution of the previous code by entering *"Sara"*, *"Juliana"* and *"Daniel"*, respectively.

Another option for defining sentinel-controlled loops is to create infinite loops and add a stop condition in the body of the *while* loop. To define this loop type, we must first understand how the Python reserved word *break* works.

9.7. Break statement

The Python reserved word **break** allows you to stop the execution of a loop at any time. If, for some reason, the program finds and executes a *break* instruction inside the body of a loop, the execution of that loop will immediately be terminated.

The following code shows the definition of an infinite loop controlled by a sentinel value *"Ohio"*, and the use of *break* to stop the loop's execution. This code represents a small trivia game where only the correct answer will allow the execution of the game to end.

On line 1, an **infinite loop** is defined (there is no condition to evaluate, it will always be *True*). Then, on line 2, the user is asked to enter the name of the US state with Columbus as its capital city. Next, on line 3, it is checked if the capital is equal to *"Ohio"*. If it is, lines 4 and 5 are executed, where the user is congratulated for answering correctly, and then the **break** line is executed (which stops the execution of the loop). If it is not, the loop is executed again. Finally, when the loop breaks, line 7 prints *"End of the program"*.

Code and execute

```
1.  while(True):
2.      capital = input("Columbus is the capital city of which US state?: ")
3.      if(capital == "Ohio"):
4.          print("Congratulations, you won the trivia!")
5.          break
6.
7.  print("End of program")
```

Note that a nested conditional was also defined within a loop in the previous program. This is very common in programming. Remember that you must be very careful when defining the corresponding indentations to ensure the program's correct operation.

9.8. Exercises

Theoretical exercises

E9.1. Analyze the following code and mention which lines of code are executed.

Analyze

```
1.  i = 1
2.  while(i < 3):
3.     print(i)
4.     i = i+1
5.  print("End of program")
```

E9.2. What are the four main parts that make up most loops?

E9.3. What does the following program print if the user enters *0*?"

Analyze

```
1.  i = int(input("Enter a number: "))
2.  while(i <= 6):
3.     print(i)
4.     i = i+3
```

Practical exercises

E9.4. Write a program that asks the user to enter a number via keyboard input. Then, create a loop that repeats as many times as the entered number (for example, if the user enters *3*, the loop should run three times). And then, within the body of loop, print four asterisks *"****"*.

Input example	Output example
3	**** **** ****

E9.5. Imagine that you are creating a system access mechanism that requires users to enter a specific keyword. Write a program with an infinite loop. Then, within the body of the loop, ask the user to enter a word via keyboard input. If the entered word is not *"Robert"*, the program should print the *"Incorrect keyword"* message, and the loop will repeat. However, if the entered word is *"Robert"*, the program should print *"Correct keyword"* and stop the loop with a *break* statement.

Input example	Output example
Party	*Incorrect keyword*
Oreo	*Incorrect keyword*
Robert	*Correct keyword*

Summary

In this chapter, we learned the basic concepts of loops in programming. We learned the main parts of most loops: (i) the initialization of the control variable, (ii) the test on the control variable, (iii) the body of the loop, and (iv) the update on the control variable. We learned the classic structure of a *while* loop. We learned how to identify common errors when defining *while* loops. And we learned how to define sentinel-controlled loops and the use of the Python reserved word *break*.

 **Cheat Sheet:** Now, we will take the Cheat Sheet and mark the tricks related to the topics learned in this chapter. Mark the following tricks with an "X": T31, T32, T33, T34, and T35.

In the next chapter, we will learn some main properties of *str* variables and some functions for manipulating text.

Chapter 10 – Strings

String manipulation is an essential part of most software programs we use daily. From websites to books to tweets, text is a form of information we encounter anywhere. Therefore, mastering the skill of string manipulation can be a superpower as it opens countless possibilities for developing different applications.

In this chapter, we will explain how *str* variables or values work, some of their main properties, and some of the most common operations.

Next, we will cover the following sections:
1. Introduction.
2. Properties of strings.
3. Getting the length of a string.
4. Extracting a character or substring from a string.
5. Searching for a character or substring in a string.
6. Other methods.
7. Loops with strings.
8. Exercises.

The code developed for this chapter is located at https://github.com/PracticalBooks/Python-For-Beginners/tree/main/Chapter10. We recommend that you develop the code by yourself to improve your coding skills. Then, in case of any issues, you can compare your code with the code available in the repository.

Remember that we suggest you create a new Colab document for each book chapter. It will allow you to keep your codes organized.

10.1. Introduction

As mentioned earlier, string manipulation is a very common process in the programs we use daily. Let's look at a few examples of its importance:
- When you search for a friend's name on Facebook, the platform compares the entered name to partially match with the names on your friends' list.
- When you log in to Gmail, the system compares that your username and password match those stored in the Gmail system.
- If you know how to manipulate text, you could extract all the information from an Excel file and manipulate it in your programs to find relevant information and perform calculations like averages, minimums, and maximums.

- Other cases include spam filters, intrusion detection systems, search engines, plagiarism detection, bioinformatics, digital forensic analysis, web scraping, and information retrieval systems.

str **Variables**

In previous chapters, we learned how to create *str* variables and values. The following code consolidates what we have learned so far. In line 1, we create an *str* variable using double quotes. In line 2, we repeat the process but with single quotes. In line 3, we show how to concatenate strings. In lines 5 and 6, we see how to print an *str* variable and an *str* value, respectively. Finally, in line 7, we see how to print variable type. In this case, the output on the screen will be *str* (see Figure 10-1).

Code and execute

```
1.  firstName = "Juliana"
2.  lastName = 'Parra'
3.  fullName = firstName + " " + lastName
4.
5.  print(fullName)
6.  print("30 years old")
7.  print(type(fullName))
```

```
Juliana Parra
30 years old
<class 'str'>
```

Figure 10-1. Execution of the previous code.

In addition to the above, *str* variables and values have interesting properties and operations that we will analyze in the next sections.

10.2. Properties of strings

Each *str* variable or *str* value in Python has three properties that we will explore in detail in this section:
1. *str* values are **composed of characters**, which are individual letters or symbols. For example, the *str* "Hello 1" is composed of 7 characters: the character "H", the character "e", the character "l", the character "l", the character "o", the character " " (a blank space), and the character "1".

2. *str* values have a **length**, which is the number of characters they contain. For example, the *str* "Hello 1" has a length of *7*.
3. Characters in an *str* appear in an ascending sequence, meaning each character has an **index number** within the *str*. Indexing in Python starts at 0. For example, for the *str* "Hello 1", the character "H" is located at index *0*, and the character "1" is located at index *6*.

Reviewing the properties of strings

Let's analyze the following code.

Analyze

1. message = "A Good Day!"

Based on the variable *message* (detailed in Figure 10-2), answer: (i) What is the length of *message*? (ii) What character is located at index 0? (iii) What character is located at index 6? and (iv) What character is located at index 10?

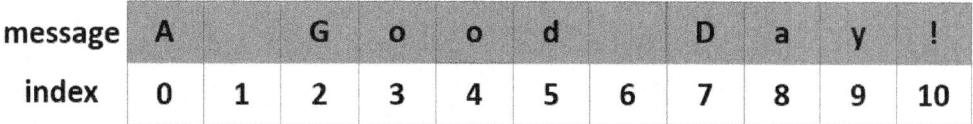

Figure 10-2. Graphic representation of the variable *message*.

Answers: (i) *11*, (ii) *A*, (iii) a blank space, and (iv) *!*.

10.3. Getting the length of a string

To obtain the length of a string, we can use the *len* function. The **len()** function takes an argument, which can be a variable containing *str* or an *str* value. It returns the number of elements (in this case, characters) that the given variable or value contains.

The following code shows how to use the *len* function to calculate the number of characters in an *str* variable and an *str* value. In line 3, we obtain the length of the value stored in the *message* variable and assign it to the variable *len1*. In line 4, we obtain the size of the value "Medellín" and assign it to the variable *len2*. Finally, the calculated lengths are printed in lines 6 and 7 (see execution in Figure 10-3).

Code and execute

1. message = "A Good Day!"
2.
3. len1 = len(message)
4. len2 = len("Medellín")
5.
6. print(len1)
7. print(len2)

⮕ 11
8

Figure 10-3. Execution of the previous code.

10.4. Extracting a character or substring from a string

First, let's see how to extract a single character and then how to extract a substring (set of characters).

Extraction of a character

To extract a character from a particular text, we must follow the next procedure. First, we use the **name of the variable** where the text is stored. Then, we open and close square brackets "**[]**", and in the middle of the brackets, we specify the **index** of the character we want to extract. This procedure will return the character at the specified index.

The following code shows how to extract various characters from a string.
- In line 2, we extract the character at index 0 of the variable *message*, which contains the letter "A", and assign it to the variable *char0*.
- In line 3, we extract the character at index 4 of the variable *message*, which contains the letter "o", and assign it to the variable *char4*.
- In line 4, we extract the character in the last index of the variable *message*. To do this, between the brackets, we first calculate the length of *message* and subtract one unit, since the last index will always be the length minus one unit (because indexes start at zero).
- Finally, the extracted characters are printed in lines 6 to 8 (see Figure 10-4).

Code and execute

1. message = "A Good Day!"
2. char0 = message[0]
3. char4 = message[4]
4. charLast = message[len(message)-1]
5.
6. print(char0)
7. print(char4)
8. print(charLast)

A
o
!

Figure 10-4. Execution of the previous code.

Analyze the following code and indicate what it would print.

Code and execute

1. brand = "Tesla"
2. char6 = brand[6]
3. print(char6)

Answer: It prints an error (*"string index out of range"*). Line 2 is incorrectly defined, as the variable *brand* does not contain a character at index 6 (the characters only go up to index 4).

Extraction of a substring

Sometimes we want to extract a specific portion or substring from a text. For example, from a very long text, we want to obtain only the portion where a product's price or store address appears (Daniel once implemented something similar in a company he worked for).

To extract a substring from a text, the following procedure must be followed: First, we use the **name of the variable** where the text is stored. Then, we open and close square brackets "**[]**", and in the middle of the brackets, we specify: (i) the **starting index** from which we want to begin extracting characters, (ii) then two dots "**:**", and (iii) the **ending index** until which we want to extract. This procedure will return the extracted substring. **Note:** Python will not include the character located at the ending index in the extraction. So, you should always define the ending index as the index of the last desired character to be extracted, plus one.

The following code shows how to extract a pair of substrings (a text label and a price):
- In line 2, we extract a substring from the variable *text* that starts from the character at index *0* up to the one at index *5* (remember that the character located in the ending index *6* is not included). In this case, we extract the substring *"Price:"* and assign it to *subString1*.
- In line 3, we extract a substring from the variable *text* that starts from the character at index *7* up to the one at index *9* (remember that the character located in the ending index *10* is not included). In this case, we extract the substring *"250"* (the product's price) and assign it to *subString2*.
- Finally, the extracted substrings are printed in lines 5 and 6 (see Figure 10-5).

Code and execute

```
1. text = "Price: 250"
2. subString1 = text[0:6]
3. subString2 = text[7:10]
4.
5. print(subString1)
6. print(subString2)
```

```
Price:
250
```
Figure 10-5. Execution of the previous code.

10.5. Searching for a character or substring in a string

Searching for characters or substrings within a text is a very common operation when working with texts. For instance, some systems inspect the messages we send on different social networks to check that the message does not contain spam (or junk content) or links to pages with viruses, among other things.

To search for a character or substring within a string, we need to use the ***find*** **method** and follow the next procedure. First, we use the **name of the variable** where the text is stored, followed by a dot ".", then we use ***find()***, and within the parentheses, we specify the substring we want to search for. This substring must be enclosed in quotes or be the name of a variable that contains another text. The *find* method will return (i) the index where the substring first appears within the text, or (ii) it will return *-1* if the substring is not found within the text.

The following code shows how to search for a couple of characters and a substring in a particular text.
- In line 2, we search for the character *"o"* within the text contained in *message*. In this case, the *find* method will return the index *3* since that's where the character *"o"* appears for the first time, and that value is assigned to the variable *indexO*.
- In line 3, we search for the substring *"Good"* within the text contained in *message*. In this case, the *find* method will return the index *2* since that's where the substring starts to appear, and that value is assigned to the variable *indexGood*.
- In line 4, we search for the character *"Z"* within the text contained in *message*. In this case, the *find* method will return *-1* since *"Z"* is not found in the text, and that value is assigned to the variable *indexZ*.
- Finally, the found indexes are printed in lines 6 to 8 (see Figure 10-6).

Code and execute

1. message = "A Good Day!"
2. indexO = message.find("o")
3. indexGood = message.find("Good")
4. indexZ = message.find("Z")
5.
6. print(indexO)
7. print(indexGood)
8. print(indexZ)

```
3
2
-1
```
Figure 10-6. Execution of the previous code.

Finally, let's analyze the following code to better understand the difference between a function and a method.

Analyze

1. message = "A Good Day!"
2. indexA = message.**find**("A")
3. **print**(indexA)
4.
5. age = 28
6. index8 = age.find(8)

In line 2 of the previous code, we observe the use of the method *find*. A **method** will always be associated with a variable or value of a particular type. There, we see that the method find is associated with the variable *message* (through a dot in the middle). The method *find* is only available for *str* values or variables. In line 6, we see how we are trying to use the *find* method with an *int* variable. If we execute the code, line 6 will generate an error since no *find* method is available for *int* values or variables. On the other hand, in line 3, we observe the use of the *print* function. A **function** is not associated with a variable or value of a particular type.

Quick discussion: To be more precise, methods must be associated with objects of a class or a particular class. The concepts of "objects" and "classes" correspond to a type of programming called "object-oriented programming" that Python supports and uses extensively. While this topic will not be covered in this book, if it is successful and readers request it, we may develop a book specifically focused on object-oriented programming in Python.

Searching for a character or substring based on a start index

In the previous examples, we saw how the *find* method received an argument (the character or substring to search for). Another variant of the *find* method receives two arguments (the first argument is the character or substring to search for, and the second argument is the start index to search from). This is used when we want to search for the second occurrence of a particular substring or character or when we use a specific index as a reference to start searching for a substring or character.

Let's look at the following example to understand how *find* works with two arguments. Suppose a supermarket worker uses the following format to store information about each product. First, they enter the product's name, then a dash "-", then the product's price, then another dash "-", and finally, the quantity available.

Analyze

productName-productPrice-productQuantity

Now, let's suppose we develop a program where that format is assigned to an *str* variable. With text manipulation and the use of *find* with two arguments, we could extract the value of the quantity for any product, regardless of the length of its name or its price (as long as the format is consistent with the example given).

The following code shows how to use the previous elements to extract the quantity of a product based on the previous format.

- In line 2, we search for the character "-" within the variable *product*. In this case, the *find* method will return index 5 since that's where the character first appears, and that value will be assigned to the variable *indexDash1*.
- In line 3, we search for the character "-" within the variable *product*, but this time starting from the previously found index plus one (+1). This means that we are searching for the second occurrence of the character "-". In this case, the *find* method will return index 9 since that's where the character appears for the second time, and that value will be assigned to the variable *indexDash2*.
- In line 4, we extract from the character in index *indexDash2+1* (i.e., from the next index after the second dash is found) to the character in the last index (i.e., *len(product)*). So, we extract the subtext *"20"* (the quantity of the product) and assign it to the variable *subStringQuantity*.
- Finally, the found indexes and the extracted subtext are printed in lines 6 to 8 (see Figure 10-7). **Note:** if desired, modify the product data (name, price, and quantity). As long as you respect the previous format, the code will always show you the quantity of the product at the end.

Code and execute

```
1.  product = "Laser-100-20"
2.  indexDash1 = product.find("-")
3.  indexDash2 = product.find("-", indexDash1+1)
4.  subStringQuantity = product[indexDash2+1:len(product)]
5.
6.  print(indexDash1)
7.  print(indexDash2)
8.  print(subStringQuantity)
```

```
5
9
20
```
Figure 10-7. Execution of the previous code.

This example teaches us how to extract various pieces of information from different texts. By practicing the previous techniques, we can analyze texts that contain thousands or even hundreds of thousands of characters and extract valuable insights from them.

10.6. Other methods

In addition to the *find* method, there are 47 other methods available for manipulating *str* variables and values. These methods are detailed in Python's official documentation, which can be found at the following link: https://docs.python.org/3/library/stdtypes.html#string-methods. While covering all these methods in this book is impossible, we'll show how some of them work in the following code. This time, try to understand what is happening and how these methods work by yourself (we leave hints in the form of comments). Then, execute the code and see the results in Figure 10-8. And if you have any questions, remember that you can use the "**discussion zone**" of the book's repository to ask for help.

Code and execute

```
1.   message = "Location: Provenza"
2.
3.   messageLower = message.lower() # returns the lowercase string
4.   print(messageLower)
5.
6.   messageUpper = message.upper() #  returns the uppercased string
7.   print(messageUpper)
8.
9.   countA = message.count("a") # returns the number of times that "a" appears
10.  print(countA)
11.
12.  newMessage = message.replace("a", "x") # returns the string replacing "a" by "x"
13.  print(newMessage)
```

```
location: provenza
LOCATION: PROVENZA
2
Locxtion: Provenzx
```
Figure 10-8. Execution of the previous code.

10.7. Loops with strings

Let's see how we can use loops to iterate through a text. The following code shows how to iterate through and display the characters of a word entered by the user (see execution in Figure 10-9).
- In line 1, we ask the user to input a word using the keyboard and assign that value to the variable *word*. For this exercise, let's assume the user inputs the *Car* word.
- In line 3, we define the control variable *i* and initialize it to *0*. This control variable will control the loop and indicates the index of the text we're currently at in each iteration. We initialize *i* to *0* since it represents the index of the first character in the inputted text.
- In line 4, we create a while loop and define its condition. This loop will run as long as *i* is less than the length of *word*. The length will vary depending on what we enter on the screen. If we continue with the example, the length of the entered text would be *3* since *Car* contains 3 characters. This means that *i* always must be less than 3 (which represents the valid indexes we can access in the entered text).
- In line 5, the body of the while loop begins. In this case, we access and print the character at index *i* from *word*. The first time the loop runs, we will access *word[0]*, which is the character "C".
- In line 6, we update the control variable. We add *1* to *i* since we want to move through all the indexes of the entered text. In this case, *i* started as *0* and now becomes *1*. Then, the code will execute line 4 again and check if the loop can be repeated.
- When *i* is *1*, line 5 will print *word[1]* (which is "*a*"). Then, *i* will increase by one and become *2*, and line 5 will print *word[2]* (which is "*r*"). Finally, *i* will increase by one again and become *3*, and the loop will end its execution.

Code and execute

1. word = input("Enter a word: ")
2.
3. i = 0
4. while(i < len(word)):
5.   print(word[i])
6.   i = i+1

```
Enter a word: Car
C
a
r
```

Figure 10-9. Execution of the previous code by entering *Car*.

10.8. Exercises

Theoretical exercises

E10.1. What does the following program print?

Analyze
1. text = "Ginza"
2. print(text[0])
3. print(text[0:3])
4. indexZ = text.find("z")
5. print(indexZ)

E10.2. What is the second argument that can be passed to the *find* method used for (when working with *str* variables or *str* values)?

E10.3. What does the following program print if *"Howdy"* is entered via keyboard?

Analyze
1. word = input()
2. print(word[len(word)-1])

Practical exercises

E10.4. Write a program that asks the user to enter a text via keyboard. Then, print the first character of that text concatenated with the last character.

Input example	Output example
Waka Waka	*Wa*

E10.5. A librarian has to analyze texts from different books. But the librarian hates analyzing texts that contain the letter "z". The librarian asks you to develop a program that informs her if a text contains any letter "z". Write a program that asks the user to enter a text through the keyboard. Then, if the text contains at least one letter "z", print "Text contains letter z" on the screen. Otherwise, print "Text does not contain letter z". **Hint:** for this exercise, you can use *count* or *find*. If you use *find*, remember that the *find* method returns *-1* if it does not find a character or substring within a text.

Input example	Output example
Pizza	Text contains letter z

E10.6. A philologist (a person who studies languages) is conducting a research to communicate with aliens. We all know that aliens do not use vowels. Therefore, the philologist wants to have a program that, when given a word, shows each letter of that word on a separate line. And if any letter corresponds to a vowel, do not show it. Write a program that asks the user to enter a word through the keyboard. Then, print each character of the word on a separate line (excluding the characters that represent vowels).

Input example	Output example
Falcon	F
	l
	c
	n

Hint: Complete all the blank lines in the following code.

Analyze

1.
2.
3.
4.   if(word[i] != "a" and word[i] != "e" and word[i] != "i" and word[i] != "o" and word[i] != "u"):
5.   print(word[i])
6.

Summary

In this chapter, we learned how to manipulate strings. We learned the main properties of strings: (i) they are composed of characters, (ii) they have a length, and (iii) the characters are stored in ascending indexes starting at zero. We learned different operations on strings, such as: (i) obtaining the length of a string with the *len* function, (ii) extracting a character from a string with square brackets "[]" and a particular index, (iii) extracting a substring from a string with square brackets "[]" and the initial and ending indexes, and (iv) searching for characters or substrings within a string using the *find* method. We learned that *str* variables and *str* values contain interesting methods we could use in our programs. And finally, we learned how to iterate over strings using loops.

 Cheat Sheet: Now, we will take the Cheat Sheet and mark the tricks related to the topics learned in this chapter. Mark the following tricks with an "X": T36, T37, T38, T39, T40, T41, T43, T44, T45, and T46.

In the next chapter, we will learn about a new type of variable called a *list*, which is essential for designing more complex programs.

Chapter 11 – Lists

As our programs grow, it is common to see the creation of dozens or hundreds of variables. But this makes the program code bigger and more complex to modify and evolve. For this problem, lists come to our rescue. A list allows us to store multiple values in a single variable, reducing the number of variables and making our programs shorter, simpler, and more understandable.

In this chapter, we will explain how lists work, some of their main properties, and some of the most common operations.

Next, we will cover the following sections:
1. Creation of lists.
2. Properties of lists.
3. Graphical representation of lists in memory.
4. Basic operations.
5. Loops with lists.
6. Exercises.

The code developed for this chapter is located at https://github.com/PracticalBooks/Python-For-Beginners/tree/main/Chapter11. We recommend that you develop the code by yourself to improve your coding skills. Then, in case of any issues, you can compare your code with the code available in the repository.

Remember that we suggest you create a new Colab document for each book chapter. It will allow you to keep your codes organized.

11.1. Creation of lists

Before creating a list, let's see the problem that lists solve. Suppose we are asked to store the ages of 100 employees of a company (that is, to store 100 integers). With what we have seen so far, we would have to create 100 variables and store in each one the age of a single employee (something like what is presented in the following code).

Analyze

1. age1 = 31
2. age2 = 25
... ...
100. age100 = 45

But, with a list, we can create a single variable that contains all 100 ages.

List creation

In Python, **lists** allow us to store multiple values assigned to a single variable. We can store letters of the alphabet, names of family members, ages, salaries, and many other things in a list. The following code shows how to define a list.

Code

1. ages = [28, 67, 40, 15]

Creating a list has a structure like the one presented in Figure 11-1.

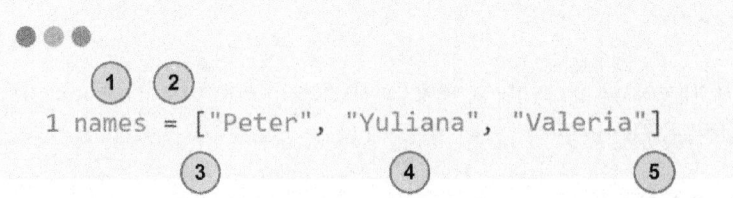

Figure 11-1. List structure.

1. The **name of a variable** is defined (usually in plural since we expect to store multiple values).
2. The equal sign "=" is used.
3. A square bracket "[" is opened.
4. The **individual values** we want to store in the list are placed and **separated by commas**.
5. And a square bracket "]" is closed.

The following code shows how to create a list that stores names and then print its contents and type. Figure 11-2 shows the output of the code execution. There we see that the list stores three *str* values, and then we see that the type of the variable *names* is *list*.

Code and execute

1. names = ["Peter", "Yuliana", "Valeria"]
2. print(names)
3. print(type(names))

```
['Peter', 'Yuliana', 'Valeria']
<class 'list'>
```
Figure 11-2. Execution of the previous code.

Lists that store different types of data

In Python, **lists** allow storing values of different types. For example, we can store a text, an integer, and a boolean, all in the same list. Although this is possible, it is generally not recommended. Instead, when we want to store values of different types, we should use a dictionary (a topic explained in the next chapter).

For now, let's see how to create a list that stores different data types. The following code defines a list that stores values of *str*, *int*, and *float* types.

Code and execute

1. myData = ["Luisa", 37, "lmalvarez33@eafit.edu.co", 164.1]
2. print(myData)

Now, think about what information each value represents. For example, what does the number *37* mean? People may say it represents a person's age, but it could represent any other value, such as body temperature in degrees Celsius. This is why dictionaries work better for these cases (but we'll cover that later).

11.2. Properties of lists

Lists in Python have three properties (very similar to those of *str*):
1. Lists are **composed of elements** (values separated by commas).
2. Lists have a **length** corresponding to the number of elements it contains.
3. Elements in a list appear in an ascending sequence, meaning each element has an **index number** within the list. Indexing in Python starts at 0.

Reviewing the properties of lists

Let's analyze the following code.

Analyze

1. names = ["Peter", "Yuliana", "Valeria"]

Based on the variable *names* (detailed in Figure 11-3), answer: (i) What is the length of *names*? (ii) What element is at index *0*? (iii) What element is at index *2*? and (iv) What is the type of the element at index *0*?

names	"Peter"	"Yuliana"	"Valeria"
index	0	1	2

Figure 11-3. Graphical representation of the variable *names*.

Answers: (i) *3*, (ii) *"Peter"*, (iii) *"Valeria"*, and (iv) *str*.

11.3. Graphical representation of lists in memory

Let's use the box diagram representation we used in previous sections to represent the variable defined in the following code.

Code

1. myData = ["Luisa", 18, 164.1]

Figure 11-4 shows the graphical representation of the previous variable *myData*. Let's analyze this figure in detail.
- The paper inside *myData* variable stores a reference with a number (an identifier). This is because *list* variables store references. A **reference** represents a location in the computer's memory where the variable data is stored.
- To differentiate references from values, the paper inside the box now contains the word *REF*, followed by a colon and an identifier.
- For the previous example (and for *list* variables in general), imagine the reference *ID: 452* as a large box that stores three small boxes inside (the list elements).
- Finally, the string *"Luisa"* is stored at index *0*, the integer *18* at index *1*, and the float *164.1* at index *2*.

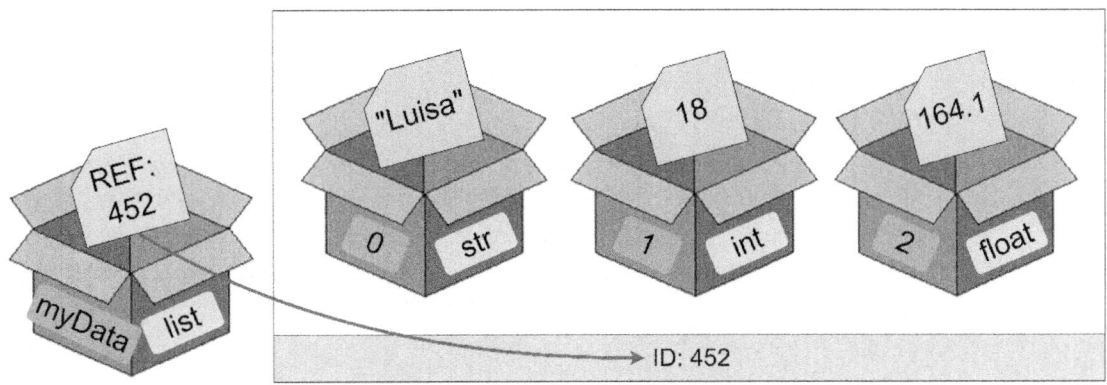

Figure 11-4. Graphical representation of the variable *myData* in memory.

Values and References

Let's look at the following code that defines two different types of variables and how those variables are stored in memory.

Code

1. age = 48
2. hobbies = ["Reading"]

Figure 11-5 shows the graphical representation in memory of both variables. In line 1, we define the variable *age*, which stores an integer. For variables of type *int*, *str*, *float*, and *bool*, **we will imagine*** that those variables store values. In line 2, we define the variable *hobbies* as a list containing a single element. For variables of type *list*, we will assume that those variables store references.

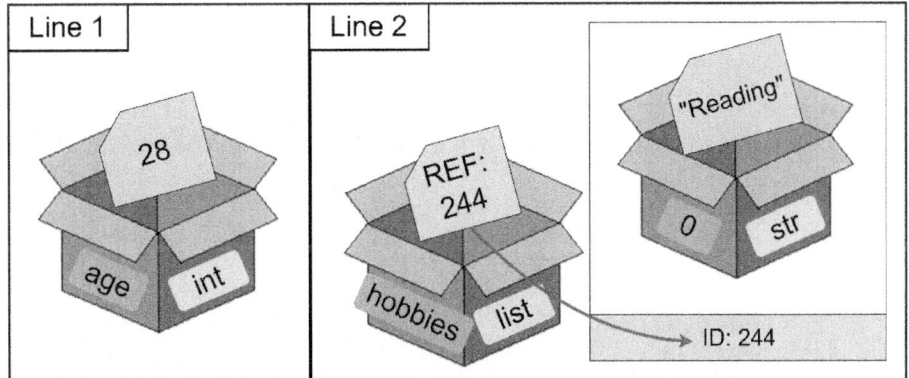

Figure 11-5. Graphical representation of the variable *age* and *hobbies* in memory.

 ***Quick discussion:** If you noticed, in the previous explanation for variables of type *int*, *str*, *float*, and *bool*, we used the word **"we will imagine"** with an asterisk. This is because this explanation is a simplification of what happens in Python. In Python, unlike other languages, all variable types store references. But in this book, we will imagine variables of type *int*, *str*, *float*, and *bool* store values. For beginner programmers, this simplifies the explanation and makes it easier to understand what is happening in the code. However, if you want to learn more about how references work for all variables in Python, you could read this article on Medium: https://medium.com/geekculture/python-reference-e6458a9a0582.

11.4. Basic operations

Next, we will analyze some basic operations for working with lists. These include: (i) accessing elements of a list, (ii) modifying elements of a list, (iii) adding elements to a list, and (iv) removing elements from a list.

Accessing elements of a list

To access an element of a list, we must follow the next procedure. First, we use the **name of the variable** where the list is stored. Then, we open and close square brackets "**[]**", and in the middle of the brackets, we specify the **index** of the element we want to access. This procedure will return the element to be accessed.

The following code shows how to access different list elements (see execution in Figure 11-6).
- In line 1, we create a list of four singers and assign it to the variable *singers*.
- In line 2, we access the singer at index *0* of the *singers* list (i.e., *"Shakira"*) and assign it to the variable *singer1*.
- In line 4, we print the length of the *singers* list (which is *4*).
- In line 5, we print the value stored in *singer1* (which is *"Shakira"*).
- In line 6, we print the singer at index *2* of the *singers* list (which is *"Feid"*).
- In line 7, we print the singer at the last index of the *singers* list (which is *"Maluma"*). Remember that to obtain the last index of a list or a text, we get the size of the list or text and subtract one.

Code and execute

1. `singers = ["Shakira", "Karol G", "Feid", "Maluma"]`
2. `singer1 = singers[0]`
3.
4. `print(len(singers))`
5. `print(singer1)`
6. `print(singers[2])`
7. `print(singers[len(singers)-1])`

```
4
Shakira
Feid
Maluma
```
Figure 11-6. Execution of the previous code.

Quickly analyze the following code and think about what it would print.

Code and execute

1. `singers = ["Blessd", "Kapla", "Miky", "Onyl"]`
2. `singer6 = singers[6]`
3. `print(singer6)`

Answer: It prints an error (*"list index out of range"*). Line 2 is incorrectly defined, as the variable *singers* does not contain an element at index *6* (the list only goes up to index 3).

Modifying elements of a list

To modify an element of a list, we must follow the next procedure. First, we use the **name of the variable** where the list is stored. Then, we open and close square brackets "**[]**". In the middle of the brackets, we specify the **index** of the element we want to modify. Then we use an equal sign "**=**", and finally, we enter the **new value** that we want to assign to that index.

The following code shows how to modify an element in a list (see execution in Figure 11-7).
- Line 1 creates a list of three motorcycle brands.
- Line 2 accesses and prints the value stored at index *0* of *motorcycles* (which is *"Honda"*).
- Line 4 modifies the motorcycle at index *0* of the list and changes its value to *"Ducati"*.

- Line 5 accesses and prints the value stored at index *0* of *motorcycles* (which is now *"Ducati"*).

Code and execute

1. motorcycles = ["Honda", "Yamaha", "Suzuki"]
2. print(motorcycles[0])
3.
4. motorcycles[0] = "Ducati"
5. print(motorcycles[0])

```
Honda
Ducati
```
Figure 11-7. Execution of the previous code.

Adding elements to a list

Adding elements is a common task, for example, you may want to add a new alien to the list of aliens (in a video game you are programming). To add an element to a list, we must use the *append* method and follow the next procedure. First, we use the **name of the variable** where the list will be stored. Then we place a dot ".". After that, we use *append()*, and inside the parentheses, we enter the **new element** to add. The *append* method allows you to add an element to the end of a specific list.

The following code shows how to add multiple elements to a list (see execution in Figure 11-8).
- In line 1, we create an empty list called *aliens* (notice that we don't put any elements between the brackets).
- In line 2, we add the value *"E.T."* to the end of aliens (in this case, it will be added to index 0 because the list was empty).
- In lines 3 to 5, we continue adding different aliens to the list.
- In line 6, we access and print the value stored at index *3* of *aliens*.

Code and execute

1. aliens = []
2. aliens.append("E.T.")
3. aliens.append("Goku")
4. aliens.append("Marvin")
5. aliens.append("Gazoo")
6. print(aliens[3])

⤷ Gazoo

Figure 11-8. Execution of the previous code.

Removing elements from a list

To remove an element from a list, we must use the *pop* method and follow the next procedure. First, we use the **name of the variable** where the list will be stored. Then we place a dot ".". After that, we use *pop()*, and inside the parentheses, we specify the **index** of the element to be removed. Once the element at that index is removed, all the following elements will move toward the previous index. For example, if we have a list with three elements (indexes 0, 1, and 2) and we remove the element from index 1, the element that was at index 2 will move to index 1.

The following code shows how to remove an element from a list (see execution in Figure 11-9).
- In line 1, we create a list with four aliens.
- In line 2, we access and print the value stored at index *1* of *aliens* (which is *"Goku"*).
- In line 3, we remove the value stored at index *1* of the list (which is *"Goku"*).
- In line 4, we access and print again the value stored at index *1* of *aliens*. This time it will display *"Marvin"* on the screen, since it was previously at index 2, but when we removed *"Goku"*, all the following values moved towards the immediate previous index.

Code and execute

1. aliens = ["E.T.", "Goku", "Marvin", "Gazoo"]
2. print(aliens[1])
3. aliens.pop(1)
4. print(aliens[1])

```
Goku
Marvin
```
Figure 11-9. Execution of the previous code.

 **TIP:** There are many other methods available to work with lists. We recommend taking a quick look at this link: https://www.w3schools.com/python/python_ref_list.asp.

11.5. Loops with lists

Once we create lists in our programs, it will be common to iterate over them to display their elements. Most programs we use daily contain lists with elements. For example, an online store may group its products into a list, and when we access its website, it will show us each product stored in that list. An online newspaper could have its news articles in a list, and it will display some of its latest news on its homepage. Other examples include music playlists on Spotify, recommended video lists on YouTube, and movie lists on Netflix.

The following code shows how to iterate through and display the elements of a list (see execution in Figure 11-10).
- In line 1, we create a list with four aliens.
- In line 3, we define the control variable *i* initialized at *0*. The control variable will serve to control the loop and also indicate which index of the list we are in each iteration. Since we want to display all list elements, we initialize the variable at *0*.
- In line 4, we create the loop and define the condition. In this case, the loop will run as long as *i* is less than the length of the *aliens* list. The size of aliens is *4*, so *i* will always have to be less than *4* (which represents valid indexes we can access in the list).
- In line 5, the body of the while loop begins. In this case, we access and print the element stored in the list aliens at index *i* (the first time it is executed, we will access *aliens[0]*, which is *"E.T."*).
- In line 6, we update the control variable. We will increase *i* by one (since we want to go through all list indexes). In this case, *i* started as *0*, and now it will be *1*. Then, the code will execute line 4 again and check if the loop can be repeated.
- When *i* is 1, line 5 will print *"Goku"*. Then, *i* will increase by one and be *2*, and line 5 will print *"Marvin"*. Then *i* will increase by one and be *3*, and line 5 will print *"Gazoo"*. And then *i* will increase by one and be *4*, and the loop will finish its execution (Figure 11-11 shows the step-by-step flow of execution).

Code and execute

1. `aliens = ["E.T.", "Goku", "Marvin", "Gazoo"]`
2.
3. `i = 0`
4. `while(i < len(aliens)):`
5.   `print(aliens[i])`
6.   `i = i+1`

```
E.T.
Goku
Marvin
Gazoo
```

Figure 11-10. Execution of the previous code.

```
1  ①         aliens = ["E.T.", "Goku", "Marvin", "Gazoo"]
2
3  ②         i = 0
4  ③ ⑥ ⑨ ⑫ ⑮ while(i < len(aliens)):
5  ④ ⑦ ⑩ ⑬     print(aliens[i])
6  ⑤ ⑧ ⑪ ⑭     i = i+1
```

Figure 11-11. Step-by-step execution flow of the previous code.

11.6. Exercises

Theoretical exercises

E11.1. What does the following program print?

Analyze

1. colors = ["Yellow", "Blue", "Red"]
2. print(len(colors))
3. print(colors[1])

E11.2. Considering the code from the previous exercise, mention which instruction should be coded if you want to remove the value *"Blue"* from the list *colors*.

E11.3. What does the following program print?

Analyze

1. colors = ["Yellow", "Blue", "Red"]
2. print(colors[len(colors)])

Practical exercises

E11.4. Write a program in which you ask the user to input four names of their favorite movies through the keyboard. Then, add each of those names to a list, and finally, print the list.

Input example	Output example
Dune	['Dune', 'Interestellar',
Interestellar	'Divergent', 'TRON']
Divergent	
TRON	

E11.5. Some aliens from another galaxy left a secret message in a Python code snippet shown below:

Analyze

1. secretMessage = ["Planet", "You", "Secret", "Are", "Zombie", "The", "Nuclear", "Alien"]

Now we need to decipher that message. To do that, take the previous list, and then iterate through the list with a loop and print to the screen only the values stored in the odd indexes of the list (i.e., 1, 3, 5, and 7). **Hint:** carefully analyze what value the control variable should start with, and how it should be changed.

Summary

In this chapter, we learned how to work with lists. We learned the main properties of lists: (i) they are composed of elements, (ii) they have a length, and (iii) elements are stored in ascending indexes starting at zero. We learned how lists are displayed in memory and the difference between values and references. We learned four basic operations when working with lists: (i) accessing an element of a list, (ii) modifying an element of a list, (iii) adding an element to a list (using the *append* method), and (iv) removing an element from a list (using the *pop* method). And finally, we learned how to iterate lists using loops.

 **Cheat Sheet:** Now, we will take the Cheat Sheet and mark the tricks related to the topics learned in this chapter. Mark the following tricks with an "X": T05, T47, T48, T49, T50, T51, T52, T53, and T54.

In the following chapter, we will learn about a new type of variable called a dictionary (*dict*), which is like lists.

Chapter 12 – Dictionaries

Dictionaries, like lists, allow you to store multiple values assigned to a single variable. The big difference is that with dictionaries, we can define positions or indexes with text. These texts will help us easily remember what we store in each index.

In this chapter, we will explain how dictionaries work, some of their main properties, and some of the most common operations.

Next, we will cover the following sections:
1. Creation of dictionaries.
2. Properties of dictionaries.
3. Graphical representation of dictionaries in memory.
4. Basic operations.
5. Loops with lists containing dictionaries.
6. Exercises.

The code developed for this chapter is located at https://github.com/PracticalBooks/Python-For-Beginners/tree/main/Chapter12. We recommend that you develop the code by yourself to improve your coding skills. Then, in case of any issues, you can compare your code with the code available in the repository.

Remember that we suggest you create a new Colab document for each book chapter. It will allow you to keep your codes organized.

12.1. Creation of dictionaries

In Python, **dictionaries** allow you to store multiple values assigned to a single variable (just like lists). In a dictionary (*dict*), we could store all the data of a person, a vehicle, or a product, among others. The big difference between dictionaries and lists is that dictionaries contain a *key/value* structure that makes organizing and accessing dictionary data easy and flexible.

The following code shows how to create a dictionary.

Code

1. myData = {
2.   "name":"Luisa",
3.   "age":18,
4.   "height":164.1
5. }

The creation of a dictionary has a structure like the one presented in Figure 12-1.

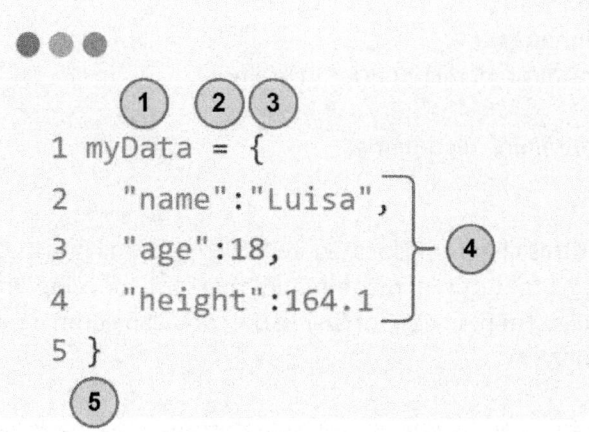

Figure 12-1. Dictionary structure.

1. The **name of a variable** is defined (which will contain the data of the dictionary).
2. The equal sign "=" is used.
3. A curly bracket "{" is opened.
4. **key:value** pairs are specified with the data we want to store, **separated by commas**.
5. And a curly bracket "}" is closed.

The following code shows how to define a dictionary that stores the data of a product and how to print its content and type. Figure 12-2 shows the output of running the code. We can see that the dictionary stores two *str* values and one *int* value, and then we can see that the type of the variable *product* is a *dict*.

Code and execute

1. product = {
2.   "name":"iPhone 14",
3.   "price":799,
4.   "color":"midnight"
5. }
6. print(product)
7. print(type(product))

```
{'name': 'iPhone 14', 'price': 799, 'color': 'midnight'}
<class 'dict'>
```
Figure 12-2. Execution of the previous code.

12.2. Properties of dictionaries

Dictionaries in Python have three properties:
1. Dictionaries are composed of a set of **key:value** pairs.
2. Dictionaries have a **length** corresponding to the number of key/value pairs it contains.
3. Key/value pairs are **not stored in a specific order**. Keys are commonly defined as text to make it easy to remember what we are storing there. However, keys could also be defined as numbers.

Reviewing the properties of dictionaries

Let's analyze the following code.

Analyze

1. artist = {"firstName":"Fernando", "lastName":"Botero", "age":90}

Based on the variable *artist*, answer the following questions: (i) What is the length of *artist*? (ii) What value is stored in the *firstName* key? (iii) How many keys are defined in *artist*? and (iv) What type of value is stored in the *age* key?

Answers: (i) *3*, (ii) *"Fernando"*, (iii) *3*, and (iv) *int*.

12.3. Graphical representation of dictionaries in memory

Let's use the box diagram representation we used in previous sections to represent the variable defined in the following code.

Code

1. myData = {"name":"Luisa", "age":18, "height":164.1}

Figure 12-3 shows the graphical representation of the previously defined variable *myData*. Let's analyze this figure in detail.
- The paper inside *myData* variable stores a reference with a number (an identifier). This is because *dict* variables store **references**.
- The string *"Luisa"* is stored in the key *name*.
- The integer *18* is stored in the key *age*.
- The float *164.1* is stored in the key *height*.

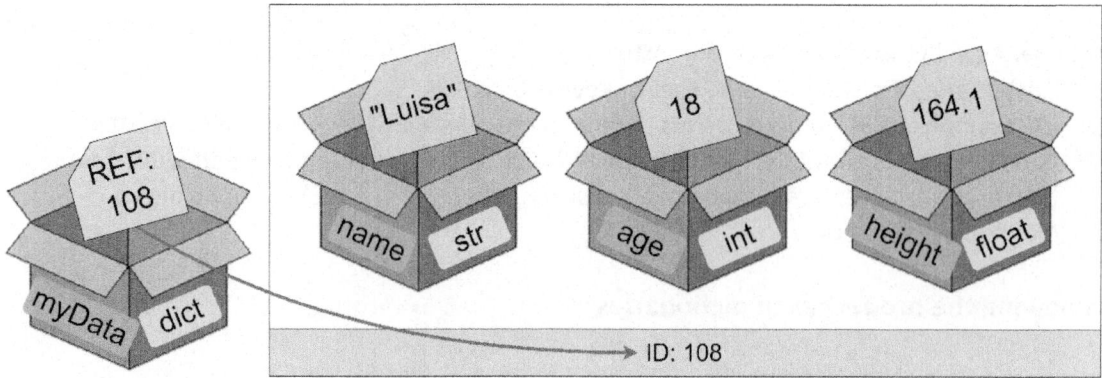

Figure 12-3. Graphical representation of the variable *myData* in memory.

When should you use a list versus a dictionary?

A **list** is best used for storing ordered data of the same type, where each element has the same meaning. Examples of this might include ages, days of the week, or grades. The following code shows three examples of lists. If we look at the list defined on line 2, we realize that all elements are of type *str*, and if we analyze the values at any index, they all have the same meaning (days of the week).

Code
1. grades = [4.5, 3.0, 5.0]
2. days = ["Monday", "Tuesday", "Wednesday"]
3. ages = [40, 12, 29, 55]

A **dictionary** is best used for storing data where the order is not important, but you want to associate the data with keys for easy access. This is useful when dealing with data of different types and meanings, such as information about a person, a vehicle, or a character in a video game. The following code shows three examples of dictionaries. If we look at the dictionary defined on line 2, we see that it contains an *str* value and an *int* value, and both values represent different things (the name and attack of the character).

Code
1. computer = {"brand":"Dell", "processor":"i7"}
2. character = {"name":"Magician", "attack":20}
3. country = {"name":"Colombia", "capitalCity":"Bogotá"}

12.4. Basic operations

Next, we will analyze some basic operations for working with dictionaries. These include: (i) accessing values of a dictionary, (ii) modifying values of a dictionary, (iii) adding values to a dictionary, and (iv) removing values from a dictionary.

To exemplify these operations, we will imagine that we are developing a video game where we customize a car.

Accessing values of a dictionary

To access a value in a dictionary, we must follow the next procedure. First, we use the **name of the variable** where the dictionary is stored. Then, we open and close square brackets "**[]**", and in the middle of the brackets, we specify the **key** associated with the value we want to access. This procedure will return the value we accessed.

The following code shows how to access different values in a dictionary (see execution in Figure 12-4).
- In lines 1 to 4, we create a dictionary with two key/value pairs and assign it to *car*.
- In line 6, we print the length of the *car* dictionary (which is *2*).
- In line 7, we access and print the value stored in the *brand* key of *car* (which is *"Toyota"*).

- In line 8, we access and print the value stored in the *color* key of *car* (which is *"Black"*).

Code and execute

1. car = {
2.   "brand":"Toyota",
3.   "color":"Black"
4. }
5.
6. print(len(car))
7. print(car["brand"])
8. print(car["color"])

```
2
Toyota
Black
```

Figure 12-4. Execution of the previous code.

Modifying values of a dictionary

To modify a value in a dictionary, we must follow the next procedure. First, we use the **name of the variable** where the dictionary is stored. Then, we open and close square brackets "**[]**". In the middle of the brackets, we specify the **key** associated with the value we want to modify. Then we use an equal sign "=" and finally, we enter the **new value** we want to assign to that key.

The following code shows how to modify a value in a dictionary (see execution in Figure 12-5).
- In lines 1 to 4, we create a dictionary with two key/value pairs and assign it to *car*.
- In line 6, we access and print the value stored in the *color* key of *car* (which is *"Black"*).
- In line 7, we modify the value stored in the *color* key of *car*, now its value will be *"Red"*.
- In line 8, we access and print again the value stored in the *color* key of *car* (this time, it is *"Red"*).

Code and execute

1. car = {
2.   "brand":"Toyota",
3.   "color":"Black"
4. }
5.
6. print(car["color"])
7. car["color"] = "Red"
8. print(car["color"])

```
Black
Red
```
Figure 12-5. Execution of the previous code.

Adding values to a dictionary

To add a value to a dictionary, we must follow the next procedure. First, we use the **name of the variable** where the dictionary is stored. Then, we open and close square brackets "**[]**". In the middle of the brackets, we enter the **new key** to which the new value we want to add will be associated. Then, we use an equal sign "=" and finally, we enter the **new value** we want to add.

The following code shows how to add a pair of keys and values to a dictionary (see execution in Figure 12-6).
- In lines 1 to 4, we create a dictionary with two key/value pairs and assign it to *car*.
- In line 6, we add the new key *"cargoBox"* with the value *"SkyBox 16"* to *car*.
- In line 7, we add the new key *"fender"* with the value *"Pocket Style"* to *car*.
- In line 8, we access and print the value stored in the key *"cargoBox"* of *car* (which is *"SkyBox 16"*).
- In line 9, we print the complete dictionary *car*.

Code and execute

1. car = {
2.   "brand":"Toyota",
3.   "color":"Black"
4. }
5.
6. car["cargoBox"] = "SkyBox 16"
7. car["fender"] = "Pocket Style"
8. print(car["cargoBox"])
9. print(car)

```
SkyBox 16
{'brand': 'Toyota', 'color': 'Black', 'cargoBox': 'SkyBox 16', 'fender': 'Pocket Style'}
```
Figure 12-6. Execution of the previous code.

Removing values from a dictionary

To remove a value from a dictionary we must use the *pop* method and follow the next procedure. First, we use the **name of the variable** where the dictionary is stored, then we place a dot ".", then we use ***pop()***, and inside the parentheses, we specify the **key** to be removed. This procedure will remove both the key and the value associated with that key.

The following code shows how to remove a value from a dictionary (see execution in Figure 12-7).
- In lines 1 to 5, we create a dictionary with three key/value pairs and assign it to *car*.
- In line 7, we print the dictionary *car*, which includes the three key/value pairs.
- In line 8, we remove the key *"cargoBox"* from the dictionary *car*, which was associated with the *"SkyBox 16"* value.
- In line 9, we print the dictionary *car*, which will now include two key/value pairs.

Code and execute

1. car = {
2.   "brand":"Toyota",
3.   "color":"Black",
4.   "cargoBox":"SkyBox 16"
5. }
6.
7. print(car)
8. car.pop("cargoBox")
9. print(car)

```
{'brand': 'Toyota', 'color': 'Black', 'cargoBox': 'SkyBox 16'}
{'brand': 'Toyota', 'color': 'Black'}
```
Figure 12-7. Execution of the previous code.

TIP: There are many other methods available to work with dictionaries. We recommend taking a quick look at this link: https://www.w3schools.com/python/python_ref_dictionary.asp.

12.5. Loops with lists containing dictionaries

In our everyday applications, programmers often create lists that contain complex data. For example, a list that includes a set of products or users represented as dictionaries. If you access your favorite online store, it is possible that the products you are viewing are internally contained in a list and iterated over to display them one by one. Next, we will explain how to create lists that contain dictionaries and how to iterate them.

Lists containing dictionaries

The following code shows how to create a list composed of dictionaries (see execution in Figure 12-8).
- In lines 1 and 2, we create two dictionaries with information about two products.
- In line 4, we create an empty list called *productList*.
- In lines 5 and 6, we add the two dictionaries to *productList*. The first dictionary will be assigned to index *0*, and the second to index *1*.

- In line 8, we print *productList*, which will display the list containing the two dictionary-type elements.
- In line 9, we print the first element (index *0*) of *productList*. In this case, it will show the data associated with the first product.
- In line 10, we print the value stored in the key *name* of the first element (index *0*) of *productList*. In this case, it will show *"Monitor"*.

Code and execute

```
1.  product1 = {"name":"Monitor", "price":119}
2.  product2 = {"name":"Mouse", "price":6}
3.
4.  productList = []
5.  productList.append(product1)
6.  productList.append(product2)
7.
8.  print(productList)
9.  print(productList[0])
10. print(productList[0]["name"])
```

```
[{'name': 'Monitor', 'price': 119}, {'name': 'Mouse', 'price': 6}]
{'name': 'Monitor', 'price': 119}
Monitor
```

Figure 12-8. Execution of the previous code.

Figures 12-9 and 12-10 show the graphical representation in memory of the dictionaries and the list created in the previous code. Figure 12-9 shows the graphical representation in memory of lines 1 and 2. In this case, two *dict* variables (*product1* and *product2*) are created and associated with memory locations that contain the data of the two dictionaries.

Figure 12-10 shows the graphical representation in memory of the complete code.
1. In line 5, *product1* is added to index *0* of *productList*. What happens here is that the paper of *product1* (the reference) is duplicated, and it is placed inside the box of index *0* of *productList*.
2. The same procedure occurs in line 6 but is applied to *product2* and index *1* of *productList*.

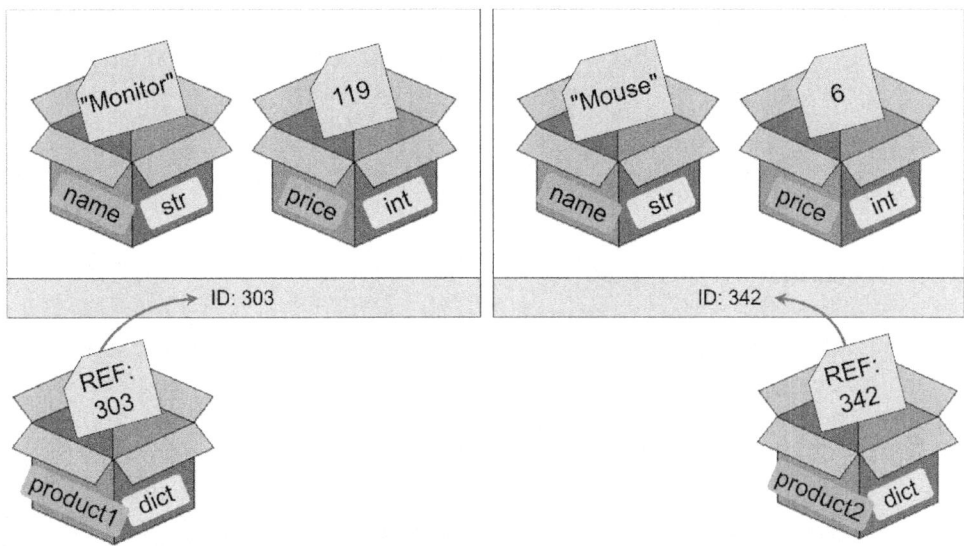

Figure 12-9. Graphical representation of the variables *product1* and *product2* (lines 1 and 2).

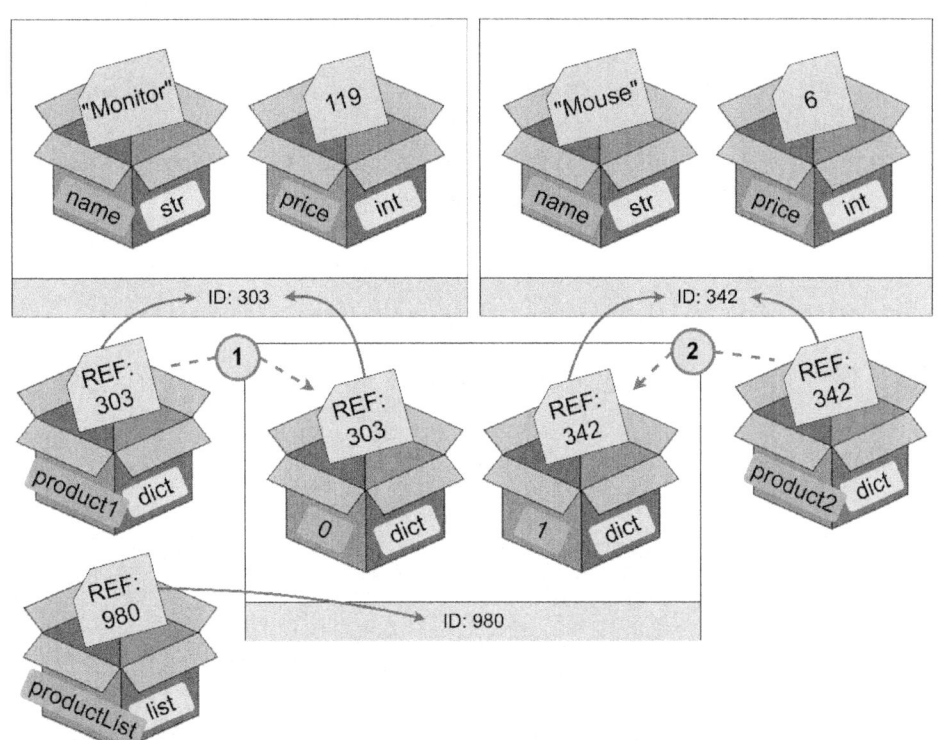

Figure 12-10. Graphical representation of all variables of the previous code.

Based on the code and graph above, answer: (i) What is the length of *productList*?, (ii) What value is in *productList[1]["price"]*?, (iii) What value is in *product2["price"]*?, (iv) What type is the variable *productList*?, (v) What type is *productList[0]*?, and (vi) What type is the value stored in *productList[1]["name"]*?

Answers: (i) *2*, (ii) *6*, (iii) *6*, (iv) *list*, (v) *dict*, and (vi) *str*.

Loops with lists containing dictionaries

Once we have defined our lists containing dictionaries, we can iterate over them and display their contents. The following code shows how to iterate over a list composed of dictionaries (see execution in Figure 12-11).

- In lines 1 and 2, we create two dictionaries with information about two products.
- In line 4, we create a list called *productList* and assign it to the two products.
- In line 6, we define the control variable *i* initialized to *0* (since we want to go through all indexes of *productList*).
- In line 7, we create the loop and define the condition. In this case, the loop will execute as long as *i* is less than the length of *productList* (less than *2*).
- In lines 8 and 9, we print the name and price of the product we are iterating over. The first time *i* will be equal to *0*, so, we will access the data of *productList[0]*, which represents the first product.
- In line 10, we perform the update of the control variable. We will increase *i* by one unit (since we want to go through all indexes of *productList*).

Code and execute

```
1.  product1 = {"name":"Monitor", "price":119}
2.  product2 = {"name":"Mouse", "price":6}
3.
4.  productList = [product1, product2]
5.
6.  i = 0
7.  while(i < len(productList)):
8.    print("Product name: "+productList[i]["name"])
9.    print("Product price: "+str(productList[i]["price"]))
10.   i = i+1
```

```
Product name: Monitor
Product price: 119
Product name: Mouse
Product price: 6
```

Figure 12-11. Execution of the previous code.

12.6. Exercises

Theoretical exercises

E12.1. What does the following program print?

Analyze
1. character = {"name":"Magician", "attack":30.5, "health":100}
2. print(character["name"])
3. print(type(character["attack"]))

E12.2. When should we use a dictionary instead of a list?

E12.3. Based on the following variable: *toy = {"name": "Train", "price":99}*, answer: (i) What type of variable is *toy*?, (ii) What type is the value stored in *toy["price"]*?, (iii) How many keys does *toy* have? And (iv) What value is stored in *toy["brand"]*?

Practical exercises

E12.4. Implement a program in which you ask the user to enter the name, age, and gender of a pet through the keyboard. Then create a dictionary with three keys: *"name"*, *"age"*, and *"gender"*, and associate each of the values received from the keyboard with those keys. Finally, print the dictionary.

Input example	Output example
Kitty	{'name': 'Kitty', 'age': 4,
4	'gender': 'Female'}
Female	

E12.5. Write a program that asks the user to enter an integer number through the keyboard. This number will represent the number of soccer teams the user is a fan of. Then, create an empty list called *teams*. Create a loop that will iterate as many times as the number entered by the user (for example, if the user enters 3, a loop that runs 3 times should be created). Now, inside the body of the loop, ask the user to enter the *name* and *country* of a team through the keyboard. Then create a dictionary with keys *"name"* and *"country"*, and associate the values received from the keyboard with those keys. Before the loop body ends, add the dictionary to *teams*. Finally, outside the loop, print the *teams* list.

Input example	Output example
2	[{'name': 'Real Madrid', 'country': 'Spain'}, {'name': 'PSG', 'country': 'France'}]
Real Madrid	
Spain	
PSG	
France	

Summary

In this chapter, we learned how to use dictionaries. We learned the main properties of dictionaries: (i) they are composed of key/value pairs, (ii) they have a length, and (iii) these key/value pairs do not appear in a specific order. We learned how to visualize dictionaries in memory and even lists that contain dictionaries. We learned four basic dictionary operations: (i) accessing a value, (ii) modifying a value, (iii) adding a key/value pair, and (iv) removing a key/value pair (using the *pop* method). Finally, we learned how to use loops to iterate through lists containing dictionaries.

 **Cheat Sheet:** Now, we will take the Cheat Sheet and mark the tricks related to the topics learned in this chapter. Mark the following tricks with an "X": T06, T55, T56, T57, T58, T59, T60, and T61.

In the next chapter, we will revisit the topic of loops and learn another way to iterate through various data using the *for* loop.

Chapter 13 – For loop

Now that we have explored how strings, lists, dictionaries, and some of their primary features work in Python, we can move on to understanding another essential concept: the *for* loop. The *for* loop is a powerful tool that offers an alternative to the *while* loop. With this type of loop, we can iterate through various types of variables and, in many cases, create more concise and readable code.

In this chapter, we will explain how the *for* loop works and how to use it to iterate some types of variables.

Next, we will cover the following sections:
1. Basic structure of a for loop.
2. Using for loop to iterate some variable types.
3. The range function.
4. Exercises.

The code developed for this chapter is located at https://github.com/PracticalBooks/Python-For-Beginners/tree/main/Chapter13. We recommend that you develop the code by yourself to improve your coding skills. Then, in case of any issues, you can compare your code with the code available in the repository.

Remember that we suggest you create a new Colab document for each book chapter. It will allow you to keep your codes organized.

13.1. Basic structure of a for loop

Before we present the classic structure of a *for* loop in Python, let's first compare the definitions of the *while* and *for* loops.

A **while** loop executes a set of instructions **while** a condition is true. On the other hand, a **for** loop executes a set of instructions **for** each element in a sequence, such as a list, dictionary, or string. As a result, **you need to specify the sequence to be iterated over** in a *for* loop.

A basic *for* loop has a structure, as shown in Figure 13-1.

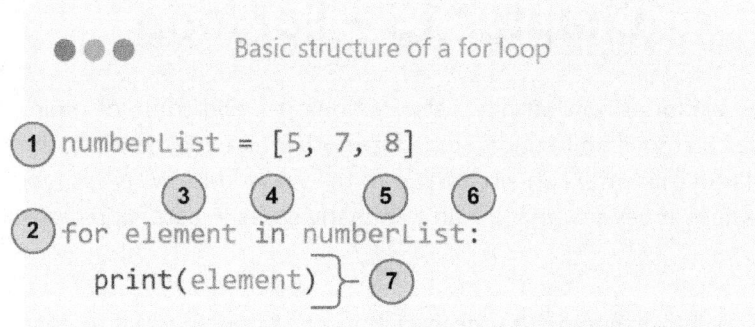

Figure 13-1. Basic structure of a *for* loop.

1. The **sequence** to be iterated is created, which can be a list, dictionary, or string.
2. In the following line, *for* keyword is used to start defining the loop.
3. Next, the **name of a control variable is defined**. This variable takes on, one by one, the values stored in the sequence. When all values in the sequence have been iterated over, the loop ends.
4. The *in* keyword is used to indicate the sequence to be iterated over.
5. The **name of the variable representing the sequence** is placed after *in*.
6. A colon ":" is used to indicate the start of the body of *for* loop.
7. The **body of *for* loop** is defined. This is where we place the instruction(s) to be executed while iterating through each element of the sequence. These instruction(s) should be indented as code blocks, moving from left to right (relative to the *for* loop) with a tab.

Programming our first *for* loop

Suppose we have a list that contains the ages of some family members, and we want to iterate over and print the values stored in that list. The following code shows how to use a *for* loop to iterate over lists (see execution in Figure 13-2).

- In line 1, we define the sequence to iterate over. In this case, it's a list of ages that contains three elements.
- In line 3, we create the *for* loop. In this case, our control variable is named *age*. We called it this way because each element in the *ages* list represents an *age*. It also specifies that *age* (the control variable) will iterate over the elements stored in the *ages* list (that's what *in ages* means).
- Line 4 contains the body of the *for* loop. In this case, we print out the value stored in the control variable *age*. The first time the for loop runs, *age* contains the first element stored in *ages*, which is *25*.
- Then, the loop is executed again, and this time *age* takes the value of the second element stored in *ages* (which is *7*) and prints it.

- Next, the loop is executed again, and this time *age* takes the value of the third element stored in *ages* (which is *39*) and prints it.
- As no more elements are left to iterate over in *ages*, the loop ends its execution, and the message on line 6 is printed (Figure 13-3 shows the step-by-step execution flow).

Code and execute

1. ages = [25, 7, 39]
2.
3. for age in ages:
4.   print(age)
5.
6. print("End of program")

```
25
7
39
End of program
```
Figure 13-2. Execution of the previous code.

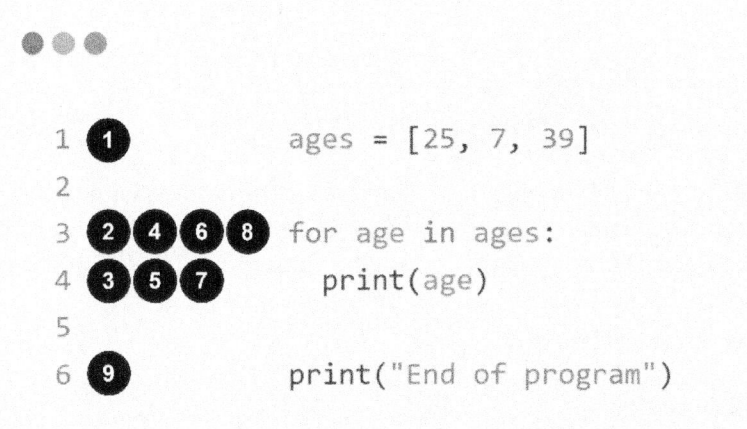

Figure 13-3. Step-by-step execution flow of the previous code.

13.2. Using for loop to iterate some variable types

In the previous section, we learned how to iterate over lists using a *for* loop. Now, let's see how to use *for* loops to iterate over strings, dictionaries, and lists that contain dictionaries.

For loop with strings

The following code shows how to iterate over an *str* variable using a *for* loop. In line 1, we create the string to iterate over (stored in the variable *message*). Then, in line 3, we define the *for* loop. In this case, the control variable *character* will iterate over and take the value of each index in the string stored in *message* (which is each character). Finally, in line 4, we print each character (see execution in Figure 13-4).

Code and execute

```
1.   message = "Hi SpaceX"
2.
3.   for character in message:
4.      print(character)
```

```
H
i

S
p
a
c
e
X
```

Figure 13-4. Execution of the previous code.

 **TIP:** The control variable of the *for* loop can be defined with any name. We suggest assigning a name that represents what is stored in each index of the sequence to be iterated. For example, if you are iterating over a list of salaries, name the control variable *"salary"*. Or, if you are iterating over a list of students, name the control variable *"student"*.

For loop with dictionaries

The following code shows how to iterate through a *dict* variable using a for loop. In line 1, we create the dictionary to be iterated through (stored in the variable *cyclist*). Then, in line 3, we define the *for* loop. In this case, the control variable *key* will take each key that exists in *cyclist* (this is how the for loop works with dictionaries, it takes the keys of the dictionary). Finally, in line 4, we print each key and the value stored in each key of *cyclist* (see execution in Figure 13-5).

Code and execute

1. cyclist = {"firstName":"Egan", "lastName":"Bernal", "team":"Ineos"}
2.
3. for key in cyclist:
4.   print(key+": "+cyclist[key])

```
firstName: Egan
lastName: Bernal
team: Ineos
```
Figure 13-5. Execution of the previous code.

For loop with lists containing dictionaries

The following code shows how to use a *for* loop to iterate over a *list* variable containing dictionaries. In lines 1 and 2, we create a couple of dictionaries (with nightclub information). Then, in line 4, we create a list called *nightclubs* and assign it the two nightclubs created previously. Then, in line 6, we define the *for* loop. In this case, the control variable *nightclub* will take the value stored in each index of *nightclubs* (it will take each nightclub dictionary). Finally, in line 7, we print the name and location of each nightclub being iterated (see execution in Figure 13-6).

Code and execute

1. nightclub1 = {"name":"Perro negro", "location":"Poblado"}
2. nightclub2 = {"name":"Teatro victoria", "location":"Poblado"}
3.
4. nightclubs = [nightclub1, nightclub2]
5.
6. for nightclub in nightclubs:
7.   print(nightclub["name"]+" - "+nightclub["location"])

```
Perro negro - Poblado
Teatro victoria - Poblado
```
Figure 13-6. Execution of the previous code.

13.3. The range function

In the previous sections, we learned how to iterate over different types of variables and values. But what if we want to use the *for* loop to print a specific sequence of numbers?

The following code shows how to use the *for* loop to print the numbers from 1 to 5. In this case, we create a list that contains the numbers from 1 to 5 and then iterate over it and print its stored values (see execution in Figure 13-7).

Code and execute

```
1. numbers = [1, 2, 3, 4, 5]
2.
3. for number in numbers:
4.    print(number)
```

```
1
2
3
4
5
```

Figure 13-7. Execution of the previous code.

What if we want to print the numbers from 1 to 100? If we follow the previous approach, we should create a list containing the numbers from 1 to 100. However, this approach would result in a lot of code. Fortunately, Python provides a function called **range** that allows us to create sequences of numbers.

Range function with a single argument

In its simplest form, the *range* function takes a single argument (an integer). If we call *range(stop)*, it will return a sequence of numbers with the following characteristics:
- By default, the sequence of numbers starts at 0.
- By default, the sequence of numbers increments by one unit at a time.
- The sequence of numbers will end before reaching the number *stop* received as an argument (which means that *stop* is not included in the sequence).

The following code shows how to use the *range* function (with a single argument) to create a sequence of numbers and iterate over it. In line 1, we define the control variable *number*, which will iterate over the sequence created by *range(6)*. *range(6)* will create a sequence of numbers starting from 0, incrementing by 1, and stopping one unit before the number *6* (which stops at *5*). Figure 13-8 shows the output on the screen.

Code and execute

1. for number in range(6):
2.   print(number)

```
0
1
2
3
4
5
```

Figure 13-8. Execution of the previous code.

But what if we want to start from a particular number or increment by two units? Let's see how the *range* function works with multiple arguments.

Range function with multiple arguments

The range function can take up to three arguments:
- **range(stop):** generates a sequence of integers from *0* to *stop* (excluding *stop*).
- **range(start, stop):** generates a sequence of integers from *start* to *stop* (excluding *stop*).
- **range(start, stop, step):** generates a sequence of integers from *start* to *stop* (excluding *stop*), incrementing or decrementing by *step*.

The following code shows how to use the *range* function (with multiple arguments) to create a sequence of numbers and iterate over it. In line 1, we define the control variable *number*, which will iterate over the sequence created by *range(1, 7, 2)*. The *range(1, 7, 2)* statement will create a sequence of numbers starting from *1*, incrementing by *2* units, and stopping before *7*. Figure 13-9 shows the output on the screen.

Code and execute

1. for number in range(1, 7, 2):
2.   print(number)

```
⇒  1
   3
   5
```

Figure 13-9. Execution of the previous code.

Based on the operation of *range*, answer: (i) What sequence does *range(0, 11, 3)* generate?, (ii) What sequence does *range(5, 21, 5)* generate?, (iii) What sequence does *range(10, 0, -1)* generate? And (iv) How should I define the range function to generate the following numbers: *2, 4, 6, 8*?

Answers: (i) *0,3,6,9*, (ii) *5,10,15,20*, (iii) *10,9,8,7,6,5,4,3,2,1*, and (iv) *range(2, 9, 2)*.

13.4. Exercises

Theoretical exercises

E13.1. What does the following program print if *4* is entered via keyboard?

Analyze
```
1.  stop = int(input())
2.  for number in range(stop):
3.      print("Rocks")
```

E13.2. What are the three arguments that the *range* function can take?

E13.3. Analyze the following code and mention which lines of code are executed.

Analyze
```
1.  groceryList = ["Bread", "Eggs", "Milk"]
2.  for item in groceryList:
3.      print(item)
```

Practical exercises

E13.4. Write three programs: (i) a *for* loop that prints the numbers one by one, from 1 to 80. (ii) a *for* loop that prints the numbers from 1000 to 0 (decrementing by 100). And (iii) a *for* loop that prints the even numbers from 2 to 66.

E13.5. A woman is looking for a name for her baby boy. A friend sends her a list of options with the following names: *"Lucas"*, *"David"*, *"Logan"* and *"Mike"*. However, the woman has had bad experiences with men whose names start with *"L"*. Write a program that asks the user to enter the four names. Then, add the four names to a list, and iterate over the list of names using a *for* loop. Inside the loop, check whether the name being iterated starts with the letter *"L"*. If so, print a message *"Name discarded"*. If not, print a message *"Possible name"*. **Hint:** remember how to extract a character from a string.

Input example	Output example
Lucas	Name discarded
David	Possible name
Logan	Name discarded
Mike	Possible name

Summary

In this chapter, we learned how to work with the *for* loop. We learned the basic structure of a *for* loop, and how to use it to iterate over strings, lists, dictionaries, and lists containing dictionaries. Additionally, we learned how to use the *range* function to generate sequences of numbers that can be used in the *for* loop.

 Cheat Sheet: Now, we will take the Cheat Sheet and mark the tricks related to the topics learned in this chapter. Mark the following tricks with an "X": T62, T63, T64, T65, T66, and T67.

In the next chapter, we will learn about the properties of functions in Python and how to define our own functions.

Chapter 14 – Functions

In programming, functions are a crucial tool for dividing the code of our programs into smaller, more manageable pieces. As programs grow larger, they can become challenging to understand, with hundreds or thousands of lines of code. By using functions, we can organize our code more effectively, making it easier to reuse and modify different program sections.

In this chapter, we will explain how functions work in Python and how to create our own functions.

Next, we will cover the following sections:
1. Values and references.
2. Creating functions.
3. Functions with parameters.
4. Scope of variables.
5. Functions with return statements.
6. Calculator.
7. Exercises.

The code developed for this chapter is located at https://github.com/PracticalBooks/Python-For-Beginners/tree/main/Chapter14. We recommend that you develop the code by yourself to improve your coding skills. Then, in case of any issues, you can compare your code with the code available in the repository.

Remember that we suggest you create a new Colab document for each book chapter. It will allow you to keep your codes organized.

14.1. Values and references

Before presenting the topic of functions, let's review the simplified way we use to imagine how values and references are stored in the computer's memory. This will help us better understand what happens when we pass values or variables to functions in Python.

Values

As we learned in previous chapters, in this book, we imagine that variables of types *int*, *str*, *float*, and *bool* store values. This means that when we assign one of these variables to another variable, **the value of the variable** on the right **will be copied** to the variable on the left. And the variables will be **"independent"** of each other. Any changes to one of these variables will not affect the other variable.

The following code shows this behavior in action (see execution in Figure 14-1).
- In line 1, we create the variable *price1* with an *int* value of *100*.
- In line 2, we create the variable *price2* and assign it the value of *price1*. At this point, **the value** of *price1* **will be copied** to *price2* (see Figure 14-2 – Line 2).
- Then, in line 3, we print *price1*, and according to "Figure 14-2 – Line 2," at this point, *price1* has a value of *100*.
- Next, in line 4, we modify the value of *price2* and assign it *200*. This change only affects *price2*.
- Finally, in line 5, we print *price1* again. According to "Figure 14-2 – Line 4," *price1* still has a value of *100* because **the variables are independent of each other**.

Code and execute

1. price1 = 100
2. price2 = price1
3. print(price1)
4. price2 = 200
5. print(price1)

```
100
100
```
Figure 14-1. Execution of the previous code.

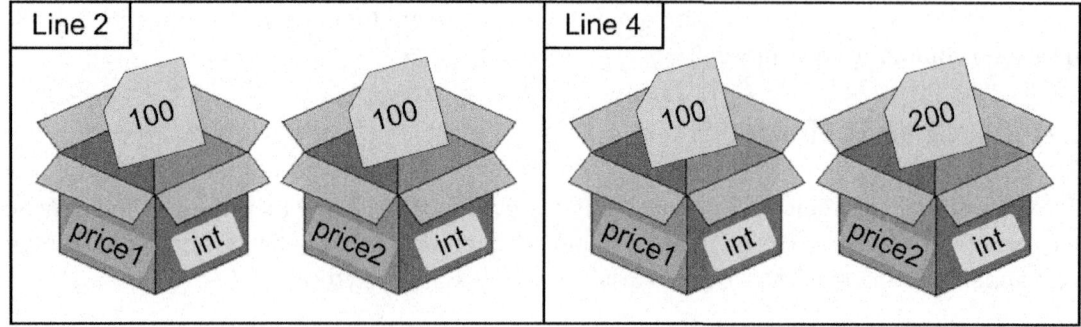

Figure 14-2. Graphical representation of the variables *price1* and *price2*.

References

As we learned in previous chapters, variables of type *list* and *dict* store references. This means that when we assign one of these variables to another variable, **the reference of the variable** on the right **will be copied** to the variable on the left. And the variables will be **"dependent"** on each other. Any changes made to either of these variables will modify the other variable (since both point to the same reference).

The following code shows this behavior in action (see execution in Figure 14-3).
- In line 1, we create the list variable *motorcycles1* with the element *"Yamaha"*.
- In line 2, we create the variable *motorcycles2* and assign it to *motorcycles1*. At this point, **the reference** stored within *motorcycles1* **will be copied** to *motorcycles2* (see Figure 14-4 – Line 2).
- Then, in line 3, we print *motorcycles1* at index *0*, and according to "Figure 14-4 – Line 2", *motorcycles1[0]* contains the value *"Yamaha"*.
- Next, in line 4, we modify *motorcycles2[0]* and assign it the value of *"Ducati"*. This change will affect *motorcycles2* and *motorcycles1* since both variables point to the same reference.
- Finally, in line 5, we print *motorcycles1* at index *0*, and according to "Figure 14-4 – Line 4", *motorcycles1[0]* now contains the value *"Ducati"* (since the variables became **dependent** on each other).

Code and execute

1. motorcycles1 = ["Yamaha"]
2. motorcycles2 = motorcycles1
3. print(motorcycles1[0])
4. motorcycles2[0] = "Ducati"
5. print(motorcycles1[0])

```
Yamaha
Ducati
```
Figure 14-3. Execution of the previous code.

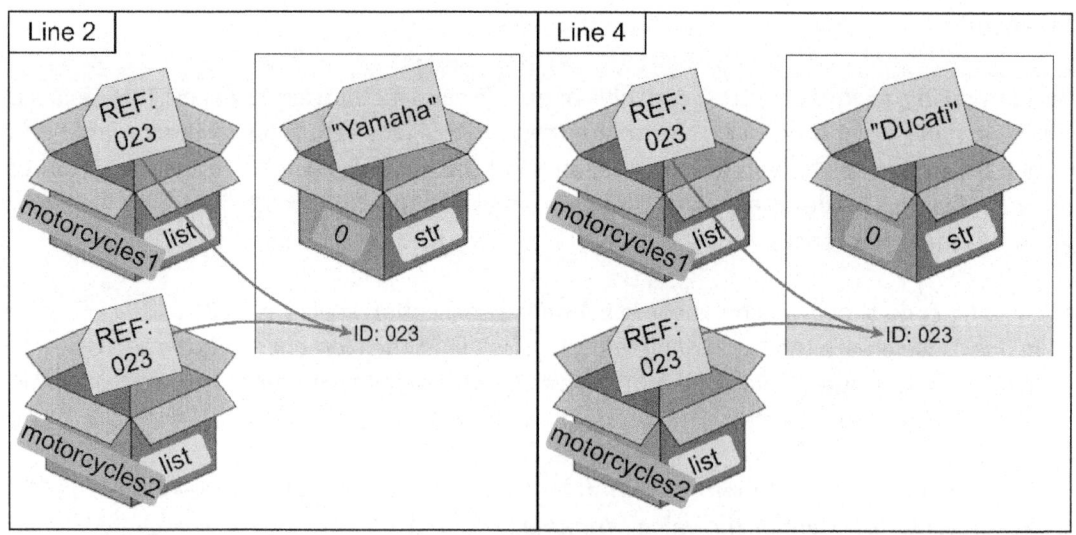

Figure 14-4. Graphical representation of the variables *motorcycles1* and *motorcycles2*.

14.2. Creating functions

So far, we hope you are already familiar with some of the functions provided by Python, such as *print*, *input*, and *len*.

A **function** is a block of code designed to perform a specific task. For example, the *input* function is designed to collect data the user enters through the keyboard. The *print* function is designed to print information on the screen. A function can also be seen as a "subprogram" used within a program.

One of the main benefits of using functions in programming is to divide an extensive program into smaller, more manageable parts. This helps to make the code more modular and easier to reuse.

In Python, we can create our own functions. To do so, we'll need to learn about the basic structure of a function.

Basic structure of a function

The basic structure of a function is presented in Figure 14-5.

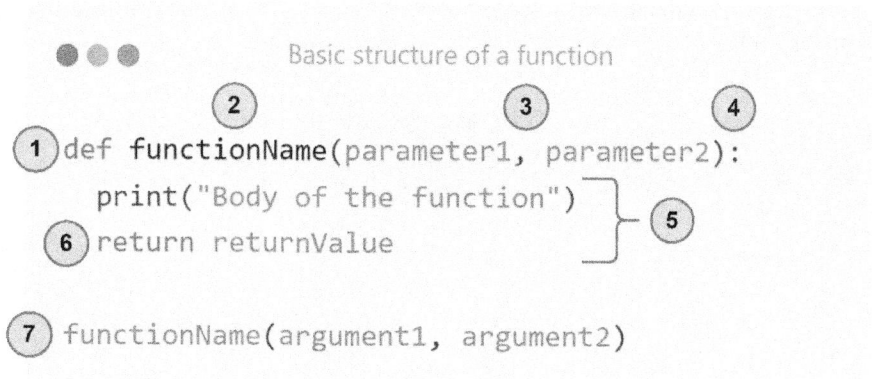

Figure 14-5. Basic structure of a function.

1. The Python reserved word **def** is used to indicate that we are defining a function.
2. We define the **name of the function**. It's recommended to choose a name that reflects the specific action the function will perform.
3. Parentheses "**()**" are added, and within them, we define the **parameters** that the function receives (separated with commas). The parameters are optional. In the next section, we will explain how functions behave with parameters.
4. A colon "**:**" is used to indicate the start of the body of the function.
5. The **body of the function** is defined. This is where we include the instruction(s) specific to the function. These instructions should be placed as indented code blocks, moving from left to right (relative to *def*) with a tab.
6. If the function has a return value, we must use the reserved Python keyword **return**, followed by **the value to be returned**. The return statement is optional and will be explained in a later section.
7. Finally, to execute the code within the function, we need to call it. To do so, we simply write the **function's name** (outside of the function's body), followed by **parentheses** and any necessary **arguments** corresponding to the function's parameters.

Creating our first function

Now that we have covered the basic structure of a function, let's create our first one. We will create a simple function with no parameters or return values. The following code shows how to create a function called *greet* that prints a greeting message (see execution in Figure 14-6):
- In line 1, we create the *greet* function, which takes no parameters.
- In lines 2 and 3, we define the body of the function. In this case, the function prints two messages.
- Then, in line 5, we call the function. This means that the body of the function will be executed, and the two messages will be printed.

- After the function finishes executing, line 6 will be executed, which prints the message *"End of program"*.

Code and execute

1. def greet():
2.   print("Welcome")
3.   print("To my program")
4.
5. greet()
6. print("End of program")

```
Welcome
To my program
End of program
```

Figure 14-6. Execution of the previous code.

Flow of execution

The flow of execution of a program containing a user-defined function differs from the execution flows we have seen in this book. So, let's examine the previous code step by step (see Figure 14-7):

- **Step 1:** Line 5 is executed. There we call the *greet* function. Lines 1 to 3 are skipped by Python (since that's where the *greet* function code is located). This means that **the code that defines a function is not executed by default**.
- **Step 2:** After the previous function call, line 1 is executed.
- **Steps 3 and 4:** The body of the *greet* function is executed, and the two messages are printed.
- **Step 5:** The body of the function ends, and now the program returns to its main execution (to line 6, the line following the function call). There, the message *"End of program"* is printed.

```
1 ❷  def greet():
2 ❸      print("Welcome")
3 ❹      print("To my program")
4
5 ❶  greet()
6 ❺  print("End of program")
```

Figure 14-7. Step-by-step execution flow of the previous code.

Exercise

Based on the following code, answer: (i) Which lines of code are executed? And (ii) What does the program print?

Code and execute

1. def greet():
2.   print("Welcome")
3.   print("To my program")
4.
5. greet()
6. greet()

Answers: (i) lines *5,1,2,3,6,1,2,3* are executed, and (ii) *Welcome To my program Welcome To my program* is printed.

14.3. Functions with parameters

Some functions require arguments or information to be passed to them when called. For example, the *range* function requires an argument to call it, which is an integer that indicates the number up to which a sequence will be created. On the other hand, some functions, such as the *greet* function, do not require any arguments to be called.

In this section, we will learn how to create **functions with parameters**, that is, functions that receive arguments when called.

The following code shows how to create a function with parameters (see execution in Figure 14-8).
- In line 1, we create the function *customGreeting* with two parameters (*firstName* and *lastName*).
- In line 2, we define the body of the function. In this case, the function prints a message with the text *"Hello"* concatenated with the values stored in the two parameters the function receives (*firstName* and *lastName*).
- Then, in line 4, we call the function and pass two arguments. The first argument is the value *"Juliana"*, which will be assigned to the parameter *firstName*. And the second argument is the value *"Correa"*, which will be assigned to the parameter *lastName*. The function body will then be executed, printing the personalized greeting.
- Finally, in line 5, we call the function again and pass two arguments. The first argument is *"Gonzalo"*, which is assigned to *firstName*. And the second argument is *"Velasquez"*, which is assigned to *lastName*. The function body will then be executed, printing the personalized greeting.

Code and execute

```
1.  def customGreeting(firstName, lastName):
2.    print("Hello "+firstName+" "+lastName)
3.
4.  customGreeting("Juliana", "Correa")
5.  customGreeting("Gonzalo", "Velasquez")
```

```
Hello Juliana Correa
Hello Gonzalo Velasquez
```
Figure 14-8. Execution of the previous code.

Error in the function call

The following code shows an error in a function call. In line 1, we create an *add* function that takes two parameters (*num1* and *num2*). These two parameters are added inside the function, and the result is printed. In line 5, we call the *add* function. However, the issue is that we fail to provide the two arguments required by the function, which causes an error message to be displayed, as shown in Figure 14-9. **Note:** Try modifying the code by passing in two arbitrary arguments to ensure it runs correctly.

Code and execute

1. def add(num1, num2):
2.   result = num1+num2
3.   print(result)
4.
5. add()

```
TypeError                                 Traceback (most recent call last)
<ipython-input-7-e945afe65805> in <cell line: 5>()
      3     print(result)
      4
----> 5 add()

TypeError: add() missing 2 required positional arguments: 'num1' and 'num2'
```

Figure 14-9. Execution of the previous code.

14.4. Scope of variables

In Python, variables have a scope. The **scope of a variable** is the section of code where it can be accessed and manipulated. There are two types of scope in Python: global and local.

A variable or parameter created or defined **inside a function** only exists in the **local scope** of that function. This means that the variable or parameter can only be accessed from within the body of that function. On the other hand, a variable created or defined **outside of all functions** exists in the **global scope**. This means that the variable can be accessed from anywhere in the code.

Local scope

To better understand how the local scope works, let's analyze the following code.

Code and execute

1. def add(num1, num2):
2.   result = num1+num2
3.   print(result)
4.
5. add(4, 6)
6. print(**result**)

The variable *result*, and the parameters *num1* and *num2* **only exist in the local scope** of the *add* function. This means that we can only manipulate these three elements within the body of the *add* function. In line 6, we try to access the variable *result*. However, if we run the code (see Figure 14-10), we will get an error message indicating that the variable *result* is not defined in that scope.

```
10
------------------------------------------------------------------------
NameError                                   Traceback (most recent call last)
<ipython-input-8-31628371015d> in <cell line: 6>()
      4
      5 add(4, 6)
----> 6 print(result)

NameError: name 'result' is not defined
```

Figure 14-10. Execution of the previous code.

Global scope

To better understand how the global scope works, let's analyze the following code that calculates the final price of a product by adding the country's taxes to its value.

Code and execute

1. def calculatePriceWithTax(price):
2.   totalPrice = price+**tax**
3.   print(totalPrice)
4.
5. tax = 10
6. calculatePriceWithTax(100)

In this case, the variable *tax* (created in line 5) **exists in the global scope**. This means that this variable can be manipulated and accessed from anywhere in the program. In line 2, we access the value of the *tax* variable without any issues, even though it is not created or defined within the function (because it is a global variable).

Figure 14-11 shows a graphical representation of the variables in the previous code, along with their respective scopes. It is important to note that the *price* parameter and the *totalPrice* variable within the *calculatePriceWithTax* function only exist while the function is being called and its body is executing. Once the execution of the function body is complete, these variables disappear.

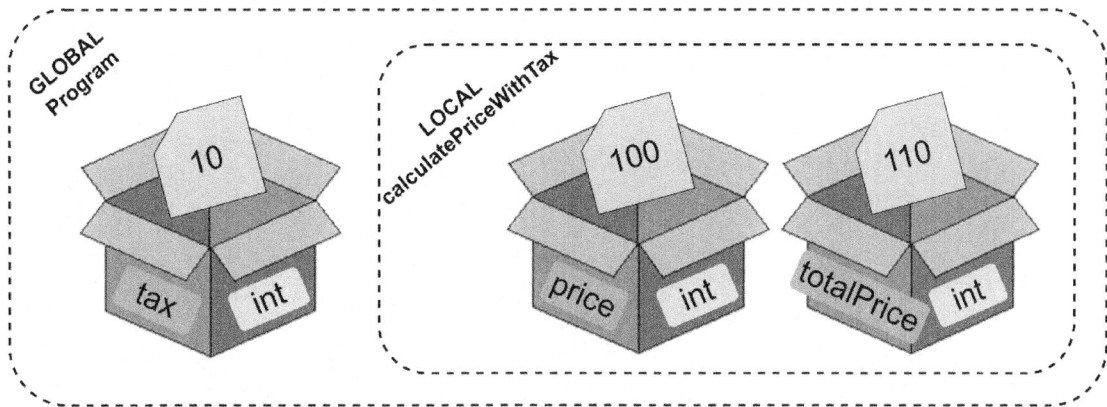

Figure 14-11. Graphical representation of the previous code variables, including their scope.

14.5. Functions with return statements

Functions can also return information to the caller. For example, the *input* function returns a string corresponding to the information entered by the user via keyboard. The *len* function returns an integer representing the number of elements in a list or the number of characters in a string.

To create a function that returns a value, we must use the **return** statement, followed by the return value, all within the function body.

For example, suppose we work in a library and are asked to create a program that calculates how much money someone must pay if they haven't returned a book on time. The following code shows how to design a function to perform that calculation based on a fictional scenario (see execution in Figure 14-12).
- In line 1, we create the *calculateFine* function that receives a parameter (the number of days the book is overdue).
- In lines 2 to 5, we define the body of the function. In this case, the function checks whether the *daysLate* parameter is greater than 7. If so, a fine of $2 is generated for each

day of delay, and that result is returned to the caller. Otherwise, a fine of $3 is generated and returned to the caller.
- Then, in line 7, we request the user to enter the days of delay in returning the book through the keyboard.
- Next, in line 8, we call the function, sending an argument (the days entered by the user, which will be assigned to the *daysLate* parameter). The result returned by the function will be assigned to the variable *fine*.
- Finally, in line 9, we print the message with the fine amount to be paid.

Code and execute

```
1.  def calculateFine(daysLate):
2.     if(daysLate > 7):
3.         return daysLate*2
4.     else:
5.         return 3
6.
7.  days = int(input("Enter the number of days late: "))
8.  fine = calculateFine(days)
9.  print("You must pay a fine of "+str(fine)+" dollars")
```

```
Enter the number of days late: 10
You must pay a fine of 20 dollars
```

Figure 14-12. Execution of the previous code by entering *10*.

14.6. Calculator

Now that we've acquired a variety of knowledge about different elements of Python, let's work on a more complex exercise.

The following code shows a calculator that can only perform addition (see execution in Figure 14-13).
- In lines 1 to 5, we define the *add* function. This will be the first operation supported by our calculator. This function asks the user to enter two numbers through the keyboard, then adds them and displays the result on the screen.
- In line 7, we define an infinite loop.
- In lines 8 to 10, we show the different operations that our calculator supports. For now, we only support two operations: *1* for add and *0* to exit.

- In line 11, we ask the user to enter the operation they want to execute.
- If the user enters *0*, lines 15 and 16 will be executed, so the program will display a goodbye message and end its execution. But if the user enters 1, the function *add* will be called, and once its execution is finished, the infinite loop will be executed again.

Code and execute

```
1.  def add():
2.      num1 = float(input("Enter first number: "))
3.      num2 = float(input("Enter second number: "))
4.      result = num1+num2
5.      print("The result is: "+str(result))
6.
7.  while(True):
8.      print("----Enter the operation----")
9.      print("1) Add")
10.     print("0) Exit")
11.     operation = int(input())
12.     if(operation == 1):
13.         add()
14.     elif(operation == 0):
15.         print("Bye =)")
16.         break
```

```
----Enter the operation----
1) Add
0) Exit
1
Enter first number: 6
Enter second number: 4
The result is: 10.0
----Enter the operation----
1) Add
0) Exit
0
Bye =)
```

Figure 14-13. Execution of the previous code by entering *1, 6, 4,* and *0*, respectively.

Let's execute the previous program a couple of times to understand how it works. And then let's continue by adding a new operation.

Subtraction operation

Let's modify the previous code so that our calculator also supports subtraction. The following code **highlights in bold** the new lines of code we added to support subtraction (see execution in Figure 14-14).
- In lines 7 to 11, we added the *subtract* function. This will be a new operation supported by our calculator. This function asks the user to input two numbers via keyboard, then subtracts them and displays the result on the screen.
- Next, in line 16, we added the corresponding text for the new operation to be displayed on the screen (*"2) Substract"*).
- Finally, in lines 21 and 22, we added the condition to call the *subtract* function when the user inputs operation 2.

Modify and execute

```
1.   def add():
2.       num1 = float(input("Enter first number: "))
3.       num2 = float(input("Enter second number: "))
4.       result = num1+num2
5.       print("The result is: "+str(result))
6.   
7.   def subtract():
8.       num1 = float(input("Enter first number: "))
9.       num2 = float(input("Enter second number: "))
10.      result = num1-num2
11.      print("The result is: "+str(result))
12.  
13.  while(True):
14.      print("----Enter the operation----")
15.      print("1) Add")
16.      print("2) Subtract")
17.      print("0) Exit")
18.      operation = int(input())
19.      if(operation == 1):
20.          add()
21.      elif(operation == 2):
22.          subtract()
23.      elif(operation == 0):
24.          print("Bye =)")
25.          break
```

```
----Enter the operation----
1) Add
2) Subtract
0) Exit
2
Enter first number: 20
Enter second number: 5
The result is: 15.0
----Enter the operation----
1) Add
2) Subtract
0) Exit
0
Bye =)
```

Figure 14-14. Execution of the previous code by entering *2, 20, 5,* and *0*, respectively.

Note: In the next section, we will have some challenges adding more operations to the calculator.

14.7. Exercises

Theoretical exercises

E14.1. Analyze the following code and answer: (i) What is the name of the created function? (ii) How many parameters does the function have? (iii) Does the function return anything? (iv) How many times is the function called? (v) What is the output on the screen?

Analyze

1. def strangeOccurrence(word):
2.   print("I saw a "+word+" last night.")
3.
4. strangeOccurrence("UFO")

E14.2. What Python keyword is used to return data from a function?

E14.3. Analyze the following code and mention which lines of code are executed.

Analyze

1. def lottery(num):
2.   if(num == 88):
3.   print("You won!!")
4.
5. lottery(67)
6. lottery(88)

Practical exercises

E14.4. Implement a function that receives a list of names and print the first name found in the list. **Hint:** complete the following code.

Analyze

1. def printFirstName(names):
2.
3.
4. names = ["Zeus", "Poseidon", "Ares"]
5. printFirstName(names)

E14.5. Implement the following additional operations to the calculator program.
- Implement an operation that allows multiplying two numbers.
- Implement an operation that allows dividing two numbers. **Note:** verify that the second number is different from zero to perform the division. If the second number is different from zero, print the result of the division. Otherwise, print *"Invalid divisor"*.
- Implement an option that allows raising a number to the square.

Summary

In this chapter, we learned about the behavior of functions in Python. We learned how to create functions and their basic structure. We learned how to create functions with parameters and return values. We learned about the two types of variable scopes in Python (global and local). And we developed a calculator on which we applied many of the concepts of this book.

 **Cheat Sheet:** Now, we will take the Cheat Sheet and mark the tricks related to the topics learned in this chapter. Mark the following tricks with an "X": T68, T69, T70, T71, T72, and T73.

In the next chapter, we will learn about three very common types of operations in programming, which we will approach using counters, accumulators, and flags.

Chapter 15 – Counters, accumulators, and flags

There are three very common types of operations when developing different programs: counting things, accumulating values, and verifying if a particular situation has occurred. For example, counting how many students failed a course (for a university program), accumulating the salary earned by each person in a company during the month to pay the payroll (for a business program), and verifying if there is any person with blood type O+ (for a hospital program).

In this chapter, we will explain how counters, accumulators, and flags work.

Next, we will cover the following sections:
1. Counters.
2. Accumulators.
3. Flags.
4. Exercises.

The code developed for this chapter is located at https://github.com/PracticalBooks/Python-For-Beginners/tree/main/Chapter15. We recommend that you develop the code by yourself to improve your coding skills. Then, in case of any issues, you can compare your code with the code available in the repository.

Remember that we suggest you create a new Colab document for each book chapter. It will allow you to keep your codes organized.

15.1. Counters

In programming, a **counter** is a variable used to track of the number of times a specific event occurs or the number of occurrences of a particular condition. We typically use a counter when we analyze multiple similar values, such as ages, salaries, or product prices.

To use a counter, we usually create a variable representing the counter and initialize it to zero. Then, we loop through the values to analyze using a loop. And within that loop, we change the counter's value by adding or subtracting a **constant value**. The most used case is to **increment the counter by one unit**.

For example, we could use counters to count: (i) how many people passed an exam, (ii) how many votes are valid, or (iii) how many computers we sold in the month, among others.

Counters with lists

The following code shows how to create and use a counter on the values of a list. The list is composed of different ages of people who work in a company, and we want to count how many people are over 30 years old (see execution in Figure 15-1).
- In line 1, we create the list *ages* containing the ages of the people in the company.
- In line 3, we create the counter called *counterOver30* (here, we will keep track of the number of people over 30 years old). We initialize the counter to 0 since we have not analyzed any age yet.
- In lines 4 to 8, we define the elements of the loop to iterate through the list of ages.
- In line 6, we define a conditional to check if the age we are iterating over exceeds *30*. If so, in line 7, we modify the value of *counterOver30* (we take its current value and increase it by one).
- When the loop execution finishes, line 10 is executed, which prints the number of people over 30 years old that we found in the list (the value of *counterOver30*).

Code and execute

```
1.   ages = [34, 50, 28, 20, 44]
2.
3.   counterOver30 = 0
4.   i = 0
5.   while(i < len(ages)):
6.      if(ages[i] > 30):
7.         counterOver30 = counterOver30+1
8.      i = i+1
9.
10.  print("Total over 30: "+str(counterOver30))
```

```
Total over 30: 3
```
Figure 15-1. Execution of the previous code.

Counters with lists containing dictionaries

The following code shows how to create and use a counter on a list containing dictionaries. The list has three dictionaries that store data for different cities, and we want to count how many cities have more than 90000 inhabitants (see execution in Figure 15-2).
- In lines 1 to 3, we define three dictionaries, each containing data for a different city.

- In line 5, we group these dictionaries into a list called *cities*.
- In line 6, we initialize a counter variable to *0*.
- In line 8, we define a *for* loop to iterate through *cities*.
- In line 9, we define a conditional to check if the population of the current city we are iterating over is greater than *90000*. If this condition is true, the counter variable is incremented by one unit in line 10.
- When the loop execution finishes, line 12 is executed, which prints the total number of cities with a population greater than 90000.

Code and execute

```
1.   city1 = {"name":"Envigado", "population":249800}
2.   city2 = {"name":"Sabaneta", "population":87981}
3.   city3 = {"name":"Rionegro", "population":147484}
4.
5.   cities = [city1, city2, city3]
6.   counter = 0
7.
8.   for city in cities:
9.       if(city["population"] > 90000):
10.          counter = counter+1
11.
12.  print("Population over 90000: " + str(counter))
```

```
Population over 90000: 2
```
Figure 15-2. Execution of the previous code.

15.2. Accumulators

In programming, an **accumulator** is a variable used to accumulate values.

To use an accumulator, we typically create a variable to represent the accumulator and initialize it to zero. Then, we loop through the values to be analyzed using a loop. And within that loop, we change the accumulator's value by adding or subtracting **the value of a variable**. That is, it is not always the same amount that is added or subtracted.

For example, we could use accumulators when we want to: (i) sum the price of all products in a purchase (to generate the invoice), (ii) sum the salary of each worker (to calculate the total payroll of the company), or (iii) accumulate savings in a piggy bank or savings account, among others.

Accumulators with lists

The following code shows how to create and use an accumulator on the values of a list. The list is composed of different salaries of people in a company, and we want to add up all the salaries to calculate the company's payroll (see execution in Figure 15-3).
- In line 1, we create the *salaries* list containing the people's salaries.
- In line 3, we create the accumulator called *salaryAccumulator* (here we will accumulate the people's salaries). We initialize the accumulator to 0 since we haven't accumulated any salary yet.
- In lines 4 to 7, we define the loop elements to iterate over *salaries*.
- In line 6, we modify the value of *salaryAccumulator* (we take its current value and add the salary value on which we are iterating).
- When the loop execution finishes, line 9 is executed, which prints the sum of the salaries.

Code and execute

```
1.  salaries = [3000, 1500, 800]
2.
3.  salaryAccumulator = 0
4.  i = 0
5.  while(i < len(salaries)):
6.      salaryAccumulator = salaryAccumulator + salaries[i]
7.      i = i+1
8.
9.  print("Total salary sum: "+str(salaryAccumulator))
```

```
Total salary sum: 5300
```
Figure 15-3. Execution of the previous code.

Accumulators with lists containing dictionaries

The following code shows how to create and use an accumulator on the values of a list containing dictionaries. The list comprises three dictionaries that store data about cities, and we want to find the average number of inhabitants in the three cities (see execution in Figure 15-4).

- In lines 1 to 3, we define three dictionaries, each with a city's data.
- In line 5, we group the cities in the list *cities*.
- In line 6, we create the accumulator with a value of *0*.
- In line 8, we define the loop to iterate through the *cities*.
- In line 9, we modify the *accumulator* by taking its current value and adding the number of inhabitants of the city we are iterating over.
- In line 11, we calculate the average number of inhabitants of the cities (we take the *accumulator* and divide its value by the number of cities).
- Finally, in line 12, we print the average number of inhabitants.

Code and execute

```
1.  city1 = {"name":"Envigado", "population":249800}
2.  city2 = {"name":"Sabaneta", "population":87981}
3.  city3 = {"name":"Rionegro", "population":147484}
4.
5.  cities = [city1, city2, city3]
6.  accumulator = 0
7.
8.  for city in cities:
9.      accumulator = accumulator + city["population"]
10.
11. average = accumulator/len(cities)
12. print("Average population: "+str(average))
```

```
Average population: 161755.0
```
Figure 15-4. Execution of the previous code.

15.3. Flags

In programming, a **flag** is a Boolean variable that checks whether a certain situation has occurred.

To use a flag, we typically define a variable representing the flag and initialize it to *False*. Then, we iterate over the values to analyze using a loop. And within that loop, if a certain situation occurs or a certain condition is met, we modify the flag's value to *True*.

For example, we could use flags to: (i) check if there is at least one person who meets the legal age requirement, (ii) check if there is a person with blood type O+, or (iii) check if a user wants to end a program, among others.

The following code shows how to create and use a flag to check if a student has obtained at least one grade higher than 4.5 (see execution in Figure 15-5).

- In line 1, we create the list *grades* that contains the student's grades.
- In line 2, we create a flag called *highGradeFlag*, indicating whether we have found a high grade (greater than *4.5*). We initialize the flag to *False* because we have not yet analyzed any grade.
- In line 4, we define the loop.
- In line 5, we check if the grade we are iterating over exceeds *4.5*. If so, we modify the flag to *True* (line 6) and stop the loop with a *break* in line 7 (since it is not necessary to continue analyzing the rest of the values in the list).
- Finally, in line 9, we check if the value of *highGradeFlag* is *True* or *False*. If the value is *True*, we display the message *"You obtained at least one high grade"* (line 10). Otherwise, we display the message *"You did not obtain high grades"* (line 12).

Code and execute

```
1.  grades = [4.0, 2.0, 1.2, 4.7, 1.7]
2.  highGradeFlag = False
3.
4.  for grade in grades:
5.      if(grade > 4.5):
6.          highGradeFlag = True
7.          break
8.
9.  if(highGradeFlag):
10.     print("You obtained at least one high grade")
11. else:
12.     print("You did not obtain high grades")
```

```
You obtained at least one high grade
```
Figure 15-5. Execution of the previous code.

15.4. Exercises

Theoretical exercises

E15.1. What is the difference between a counter and an accumulator?

E15.2. Analyze the following code and mention which lines of code are executed.

Analyze
1. ages = [20, 10, 29]
2.
3. for age in ages:
4.   if(age < 15):
5.   break
6.   print(age)

Practical exercises

E15.3. NASA hires you to analyze a list of asteroids and count how many have a high probability of colliding with Earth (those located at a distance less than 4660283 miles). NASA provides you with a list of asteroids, which internally contains the name and distance of each asteroid. Reuse the following code to count how many asteroids have a high collision probability.

Analyze
1. a1 = {"name":"2022 HX1", "distance":1547214}
2. a2 = {"name":"2022 HA2", "distance":2870734}
3. a3 = {"name":"101955 Bennu", "distance":20188350}
4. asteroids = [a1, a2, a3]

E15.4. Based on the previous code, display on the screen the average distance of all the asteroids in the list provided by NASA.

Summary

In this chapter, we explored the concepts of counters, accumulators, and flags and how they can be used to perform various operations. We learned that counters are variables used for counting things. We learned that accumulators are variables used for accumulating values. And we learned that flags are Boolean variables used to check if a certain situation has occurred.

 **Cheat Sheet:** Now, we will take the Cheat Sheet and mark the tricks related to the topics learned in this chapter. Mark the following tricks with an "X": T74, T75, T76, T77, T78, and T79.

In the next chapter, we will learn how to manipulate files and analyze their data.

Chapter 16 – Files

So far, we have used variables to store data in our programs. However, variables only allow storing that data in the computer's memory while the program is running. If the program ends its execution, all that data disappears (it does not persist).

In this chapter, we will explain how to use files to persist our program's data (even after our programs end their execution).

Next, we will cover the following sections:
1. Introduction.
2. Creating and opening files.
3. Reading information from files.
4. Writing information to files.
5. Datasets.
6. Exercises.

The code developed for this chapter is located at https://github.com/PracticalBooks/Python-For-Beginners/tree/main/Chapter16. We recommend that you develop the code by yourself to improve your coding skills. Then, in case of any issues, you can compare your code with the code available in the repository.

Remember that we suggest you create a new Colab document for each book chapter. It will allow you to keep your codes organized.

16.1. Introduction

As we saw earlier, variables don't allow us to persist information. If we want our program's data to persist even after the program ends its execution, we can achieve this by using **files**.

Many programs store their information in files or similar managers, commonly known as databases. Examples include social network data, purchases made in an online store, payroll information for a company, and characters acquired in a video game, among others.

Learning how to manipulate files will be useful for persisting data in our programs. Additionally, we can use this knowledge to analyze data we find online or collect through other means. For example, we can analyze Twitter trends, weather data, traffic data, socioeconomic data, literary works, and many others.

Figure 16-1 shows a spreadsheet excerpt containing information on some of the 2000 most popular songs on Spotify from 1998 to 2020. With the techniques we learn in this chapter, we can manipulate this data to perform operations such as finding the artists with the most songs, finding the most popular genres, finding the average duration of these songs, showing the most popular songs in 2015, and many more. Remember that these methods are not limited to this file and data type; as a programmer, you can apply them to any field and type of information you work with.

	A	B	C	D	E	F
1	artist	song	duration_ms	genre	year	popularity
2	Britney Spear	Oops!...I Did It Again	211160	pop	2000	77
3	blink-182	All The Small Things	167066	rock, pop	1999	79
4	Faith Hill	Breathe	250546	pop, country	1999	66
5	Bon Jovi	It's My Life	224493	rock, metal	2000	78
6	*NSYNC	Bye Bye Bye	200560	pop	2000	65
7	Sisqo	Thong Song	253733	hip hop, pop,	1999	69
8	Eminem	The Real Slim Shady	284200	hip hop	2000	86
9	Robbie Willia	Rock DJ	258560	pop, rock	2000	68
10	Destiny's Chil	Say My Name	271333	pop, R&B	1999	75
11	Modjo	Lady - Hear Me Tonigh	307153	Dance/Electr	2001	77
12	Gigi D'Agostir	L'Amour Toujours	238759	pop	2011	1
13	Eiffel 65	Move Your Body - Gab	268863	pop	1999	56
14	Bomfunk MC'	Freestyler	306333	pop	2000	55
15	Sting	Desert Rose	285960	rock, pop	1999	62
16	Melanie C	Never Be The Same Ag	294200	pop, Dance/E	1999	61
17	Aaliyah	Try Again	284000	hip hop, pop,	2002	53
18	Anastacia	I'm Outta Love - Radio	245400	pop	1999	64
19	Alice Deejay	Better Off Alone	214883	pop	2000	73
20	Gigi D'Agostir	The Riddle	285426	pop	1999	64

songs_normalize

Figure 16-1. Extract from a spreadsheet of popular songs on Spotify.

16.2. Creating and opening files

Suppose we want to create and manipulate a file where we store information about the money we save weekly. Before using this information, we must create a file.

Figures 16-2 and 16-3 show the steps we must follow to create a file in Colab.
1. We access a Colab document and click on the "folder" icon in the left-hand menu. This action opens a section called "Files," where we can see some folders and files that the Colab runtime environment can access.
2. Then, under the *sample_data* folder, right-click and select the *"New file"* option.
3. Rename the file and name it *savings.txt*
4. Then, double-click on the *savings.txt* file and copy the values *150,30,1200* into it (wait a couple of seconds for the file to be automatically saved).

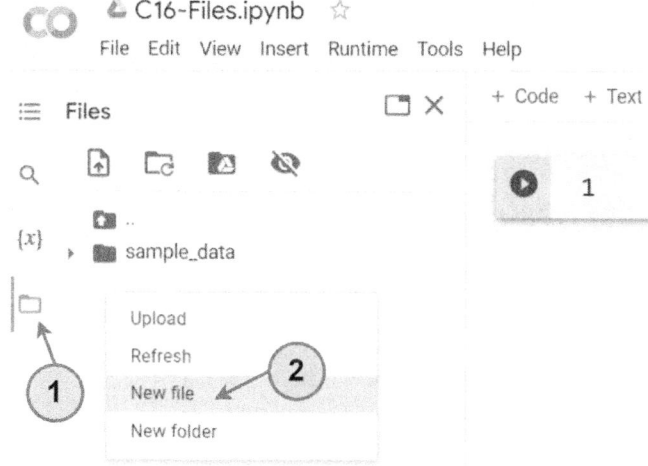

Figure 16-2. Steps 1 and 2 for creating a file in Colab.

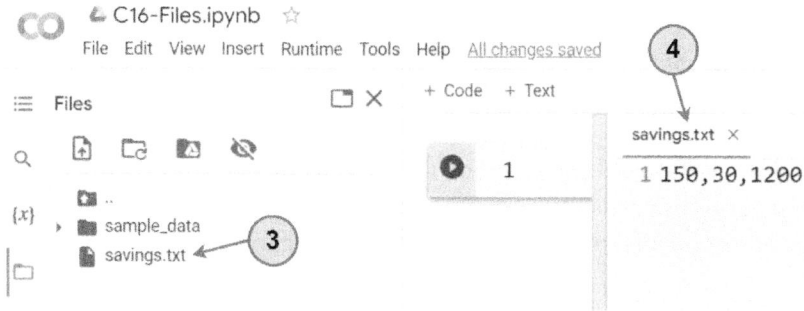

Figure 16-3. Steps 3 and 4 for creating a file in Colab.

We assume that the values *150*, *30*, and *1200* stored in the *savings.txt* file represent the amount of money saved during weeks 1, 2, and 3, respectively.

 **Quick discussion:** The files created in Colab following the above steps only persist as long as the Colab runtime environment is active. These files will be deleted if you close the browser or turn off the computer. However, you can read this article where we show you how to connect Colab files to Google Drive documents so that the files are never deleted, and the information persists: https://bit.ly/ColabDriveTutorial.

Opening a file

Now that we have created our *savings.txt* file let's see how to open it from our Python code. The following code shows how to open the *savings.txt* file using the **open()** function, which takes the file name as an argument. The opened file with all its information is assigned to the *savingsFile* variable. This variable will be of type "*_io.TextIOWrapper*", which is a built-in file handling type in Python. If we execute the code and do not encounter any errors, we have successfully opened the file.

Code and execute

1. savingsFile = open("savings.txt")

Now that we have learned how to create and open files, let's see how to read information from those files in the next section.

16.3. Reading information from files

To read the information contained in a file, we simply use the variable that represents the file and then call the *read* method. The **read** method will return a string with the entire file contents.

The following code shows how to read information from a file (see execution in Figure 16-4). In line 1, we open the *savings.txt* file. In line 2, we read the content of the *savings.txt* file using the *read* method and store the information in the *content* variable. Finally, in line 4, we print *content*.

Code and execute

1. savingsFile = open("savings.txt")
2. content = **savingsFile.read()**
3.
4. print(content)

```
150,30,1200
```
Figure 16-4. Execution of the previous code.

Separate information by commas

As we've seen, we separated the savings information using commas. We used the comma as a separator, which in programming is known as a **delimiter**. It's common for information in many programs we use daily to be stored with delimiters. The comma "," and semicolon ";" are two of the most popular delimiters. For example, in Excel, a user can store a document in CSV format, which stands for "comma-separated values." However, a programmer can define any delimiter they want.

Now let's see how to split information from a file. The following code shows how to read and split the information from a file (see execution in Figure 16-5).
- Lines 1 and 2 were discussed in the previous example.
- In line 3, we invoke the **split** method over the *content* variable. The *split* method receives an argument (a delimiter), and it is responsible for dividing a string according to the delimiter and returning a list with the separated elements (assigned to the variable *savings*). Since *content* contains three values separated by commas, this line will create a list with the three separated values.
- In line 5, we print the *savings* list.
- In line 6, we print the length of *savings*, which is *3*.
- Finally, in line 7, we access and print *savings[0]*, which is *150*.

Code and execute

1. savingsFile = open("savings.txt")
2. content = savingsFile.read()
3. savings = **content.split(",")**
4.
5. print(savings)
6. print(len(savings))
7. print(savings[0])

```
['150', '30', '1200']
3
150
```
Figure 16-5. Execution of the previous code.

Line-by-line reading

When we work with large amounts of data, it's common to divide the information stored in a file into lines. For example, if we have a customer system, we could store each customer's information on a separate line in a file. The data for the first customer would be on the first line of the file, the data for the second customer on the second line of the file, and so on.

Let's create a file called *customers.txt* with the following content (see Figure 16-6). This file stores information for different customers separated by lines. Each line includes their firstName, lastName, and age.

customers.txt File

1. Juan,Meneses,41
2. Alejandra,Uribe,24
3. Gerardo,Cartagena,30

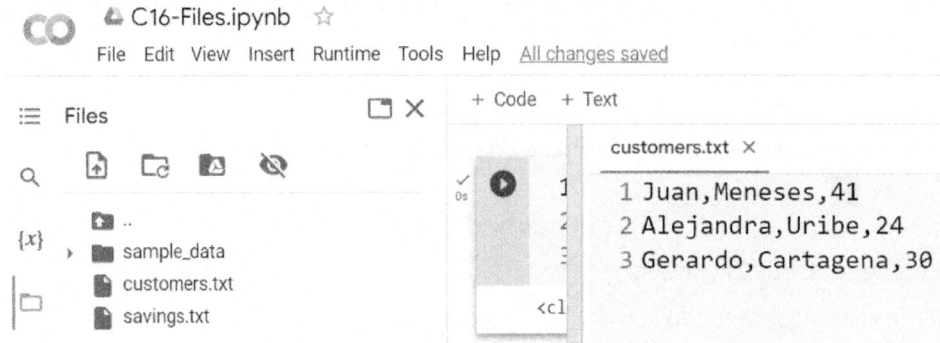

Figure 16-6. *customers.txt* File in Colab.

The following code shows how to read the information contained in the previous file (see execution in Figure 16-7).
- In line 1, we open the file *customers.txt* and assign it to the variable *file*.
- In line 2, we read the content of the *customers.txt* file, but this time by lines, using the *readlines* method. The *readlines* method returns a list where each index represents a line of the file we read (we assign that list to *content*). In this case, at index 0 of *content* will be the content of the first line of *customers.txt* (*Juan,Meneses,41*).
- In line 4, we iterate over *content* with a *for* loop. In the first iteration, the variable *line* will be associated with the first line of the file.
- In line 5, we modify the *line* variable using the *strip* method, which removes any leading or trailing whitespace.
- In line 6, we invoke the *split* method over the variable *line*. This time split will return a list where index 0 contains the customer's first name, index 1 contains the customer's last, and index 2 contains the customer's age.
- In lines 7 to 9, we print the customer's data from the first line.
- Then, the loop runs again as many lines as in the *customers.txt* file. In this case, it runs three times.

Code and execute

1. file = open("customers.txt")
2. content = file.readlines()
3.
4. for line in content:
5.   line = line.strip()
6.   customerData = line.split(",")
7.   print("First Name: "+customerData[0])
8.   print("Last Name: "+customerData[1])
9.   print("Age: "+customerData[2])

```
First Name: Juan
Last Name: Meneses
Age: 41
First Name: Alejandra
Last Name: Uribe
Age: 24
First Name: Gerardo
Last Name: Cartagena
Age: 30
```
Figure 16-7. Execution of the previous code.

16.4. Writing information to files

To write information to files we must make a variation using the *open* function and two new methods: *write* and *close*. The following code shows how to write information to a file (see execution in Figure 16-8).

- In line 1, we use the *open* function to open the *savings.txt* file.
- In line 2, we read the complete content of the *savings.txt* file and assign it to the variable *content*.
- In line 4, we open the *savings.txt* file again with the *open* function. This time, we pass a second argument to the *open* function ("w"). This argument indicates that we are opening the file in write mode this time, and we assign it to the variable *savingsFileW*.
- In line 5, we ask the user to enter a new saving and assign it to the variable *newSaving*.
- In line 6, we concatenate the current content of the *savings.txt* file with the text "," (which separates the previous savings from the new saving), and finally, with the new saving entered by the user.

- In line 8, we use the *write* method over the variable *savingsFileW* and send it an argument (*newContent*). The **write** method overwrites all previous content of the file and replaces it with the content of the *newContent* variable.
- Since we opened the file in write mode, we must close the file on line 9 using the **close** method over the variable *savingsFileW*.

Code and execute

1. savingsFile = open("savings.txt")
2. content = savingsFile.read()
3.
4. savingsFileW = open("savings.txt", "w")
5. newSaving = input("Enter your savings for the week: ")
6. newContent = content + "," + newSaving
7.
8. savingsFileW.write(newContent)
9. savingsFileW.close()

```
Enter your savings for the week: 300
```
Figure 16-8. Execution of the previous code by entering *300*.

If we execute the previous code and enter a saving value, the program will modify the *savings.txt* file and add the entered value to the end of the file. Next, close and reopen the *savings.txt* file in Colab to identify the changes.

Quick discussion: The *open* function provides other values that can be sent as the second argument (in addition to *"w"*). For example, *"a"* indicates that the file is opened for writing and that the new content will be added to the end of the file. The advantage of *"w"* over *"a"* is that *"w"* allows us to modify the file entirely, not just add information to the end of it. You can find more details on the *open* function at the following link: https://docs.python.org/3/library/functions.html#open.

16.5. Datasets

A **dataset** is a collection of data typically organized in a tabular form or separated by a specific character (a delimiter). Each dataset column represents a variable, and each row corresponds to a particular element for which store information. For example, a row could correspond to data about a person, a patient, a product, a song, and so on.

Next, we will use a dataset with information on some of the top 2000 most popular songs on Spotify from the last 20 years. First, download the following file to your computer: https://bit.ly/songsCSV (taken from: https://www.kaggle.com/datasets/paradisejoy/top-hits-spotify-from-20002019) and then follow the steps in Figure 16-9.
1. Drag the *songs.csv* file (downloaded from the previous link) to the *"Files"* section of Colab.
2. Double-click on the *songs.csv* file, and you will be able to see the file's contents with information on the songs.

Figure 16-9. Uploading the *songs.csv* file to Colab.

Reading data from the dataset

Now let's read the data from the dataset. The following code shows how to read and display the names of the songs stored in the dataset (see the execution excerpt in Figure 16-10).
- In line 1, we open the *songs.csv* file and assign it to the variable *file*.
- In line 2, we read the contents of the songs file by lines and assign it to the variable *content*.
- In line 4, we create the control variable *i* of the loop. This time we initialize *i* to *1* since we will skip index 0 because that is where the line containing the column headers is located.

- In lines 5 to 9, we implement the loop, remove any leading or trailing whitespace, separate the line text by commas, and finally access and display the index 1 of *songData* (corresponding to the name of the song in each line).

Code and execute

```
1.  file = open("songs.csv")
2.  content = file.readlines()
3.
4.  i = 1
5.  while(i < len(content)):
6.      line = content[i].strip()
7.      songData = line.split(",")
8.      print(songData[1])
9.      i = i+1
```

```
Cruel Summer
The Git Up
Dancing With A Stranger (with Normani)
Circles
```
Figure 16-10. Excerpt of the previous code execution.

16.6. Exercises

Theoretical exercises

E16.1. What is the *read* method used for in Python file handling?

E16.2. What is the *readlines* method used for in Python file handling?

Practical exercises

E16.3. Based on this chapter's song dataset (*songs.csv*), implement the following exercises as individual programs.
- Write a program that displays the names of songs released in 2000. **Hint:** you could use the following statement inside the loop body: *if(int(songData[4]) == 2000):*
- Write a program that displays the names of songs by the artist *"Eminem"*.
- Write a program that displays the names of songs that start with the letter *"D"*.

- Write a program that displays how many songs have a duration of more than *400000* milliseconds.
- Write a program that displays the average popularity of all songs.

Summary

In this chapter, we learned how to manipulate files. We learned how to create files in Colab to store data. We learned how to open files using the *open* function. We learned how to read complete files using the *read* method and files by lines using *readlines*. We learned how to open files in write mode and write information using the *write* method. Finally, we learned how to manipulate datasets.

 **Cheat Sheet:** Now, we will take the Cheat Sheet and mark the tricks related to the topics learned in this chapter. Mark the following tricks with an "X": T42, T80, T81, T82, T83, T84, and T85.

In the next chapter, we will learn how to use libraries in Python, including Matplotlib.

Chapter 17 – Libraries – Matplotlib

In the previous chapters, we learned how to use different types of variables, elements, and functions that Python provides. But Python also provides a standard library containing multiple modules and additional components for developing different programs. There is even a Python package index with hundreds of thousands of components to develop diverse types of programs.

In this chapter, we will present a brief introduction to libraries in Python, and we will learn how to use some of them.

Next, we will cover the following sections:
1. Introduction.
2. The Python Standard Library.
3. The Python Package Index (PyPI).
4. Introduction to Matplotlib.
5. Exercises.

The code developed for this chapter is located at https://github.com/PracticalBooks/Python-For-Beginners/tree/main/Chapter17. We recommend that you develop the code by yourself to improve your coding skills. Then, in case of any issues, you can compare your code with the code available in the repository.

Remember that we suggest you create a new Colab document for each book chapter. It will allow you to keep your codes organized.

17.1. Introduction

A **library** is a collection of pre-written code modules that can be imported and used in a Python program. A library provides a set of functions, classes, and variables that can be utilized in our programs to simplify and speed up the development process of a program.

Next, we will explore some Python libraries, including a default library included with Python and some popular third-party libraries developed by the Python community.

17.2. The Python Standard Library

The **Python Standard Library** is a collection of modules included with Python by default, without requiring additional installations or downloads (https://docs.python.org/3/library/index.html). This library includes modules to manage files and directories, handle dates and times, perform mathematical calculations, and much more. By using this library, a programmer can save time and focus on developing their own programs without having to "reinvent the wheel".

In this section, we will examine two of the most used modules of "The Python Standard Library": *math* and *random*.

math module

This module provides access to a set of mathematical functions (https://docs.python.org/3/library/math.html).

The following code shows how to use a couple of functions of this module (see execution in Figure 17-1).
- In line 1, we use the Python reserved keyword ***import*** to indicate that we want to use a module. Then we add the module's name to import (in this case, *math*).
- In line 3, we use the *sqrt* function from the *math* module. The *sqrt* function takes an argument, calculates the square root of that argument, and returns the result.
- In line 4, we use the *fabs* function, which calculates the absolute value of the received argument and returns the result.

Code and execute

1. import math
2.
3. print(math.sqrt(16))
4. print(math.fabs(-8))

```
4.0
8.0
```
Figure 17-1. Execution of the previous code.

random module

This module provides functions for generating random numbers, random selections, and random sequences (https://docs.python.org/3/library/random.html).

The following code shows how to use a couple of functions of this module (see the random execution in Figure 17-2).
- In line 1, we import the *random* module.

- In line 3, we call the *randint* function from the *random* module. This function takes two arguments (two integers) and returns a random integer between these numbers.
- In line 4, we print the generated random number.
- In line 6, we create a list of candidates for a draw.
- In line 7, we call the *choice* function from the *random* module. This function takes a sequence (in this case, a list) and returns a random element from the list.

Code and execute

```
1. import random
2.
3. randomNumber = random.randint(1, 10)
4. print(randomNumber)
5.
6. candidates = ["Jhair", "Harold", "Jeison", "Juan"]
7. print(random.choice(candidates))
```

```
6
Harold
```

Figure 17-2. Random execution of the previous code.

17.3. The Python Package Index (PyPI)

PyPI is a repository that hosts thousands of Python packages, libraries, and modules developed and contributed by the Python community (https://pypi.org/). PyPI contains over 400,000 projects and more than 600,000 users.

Let's look at some popular PyPI projects that you could use to develop different programs:
- **PyGame:** library for developing video games.
- **Django:** library for developing web applications.
- **Matplotlib:** library for generating visualizations and graphs.
- **Pillow:** library for manipulating and processing images.
- **NumPy:** library for numerical computing and data analysis.

Next, we will see how to use the Matplotlib library.

17.4. Introduction to Matplotlib

Matplotlib is a popular library for creating static, interactive, and animated visualizations in Python. It provides a wide range of tools for creating various types of graphs, charts, plots, and other visual representations of data (https://matplotlib.org/). Matplotlib is available through PyPI (https://pypi.org/project/matplotlib/) and was created in 2003 by John D. Hunter. This library showcases the impact the Python community can have through its collaborative development efforts.

Matplotlib is not part of the "Python Standard Library," meaning it must be installed before it can be used. However, due to its popularity, Matplotlib comes pre-installed in Colab.

In this section, we will explore one of the most popular modules of Matplotlib called *PyPlot*, and some of its most popular functions.

PyPlot plot function

PyPlot is a module that provides several functions for creating different types of plots, such as line plots, scatter plots, bar plots, histograms, and many more. In this section, we will focus on the *plot* function.

The function *plot* receives two arguments (two lists, *x* and *y*), and draws a polygon with vertices given by the coordinates of the *x* list on the X-axis (horizontal), and the coordinates of the *y* list on the Y-axis (vertical). The following code shows how to use the *plot* function (see execution in Figure 17-3):

- In line 1, we import the *PyPlot* module from *matplotlib.pyplot* and assign it the alias *plt* using the *as* keyword. The alias is a short name that allows us to use the module directly with the name *plt*, rather than the original long version *matplotlib.pyplot*.
- In line 4, we create a list *x* to simulate the years we have saved money. This list will be used as the X-axis of our graph.
- In line 6, we create a list *y* to simulate the money saved each year. This list will be used as the Y-axis of our graph.
- In line 8, we use the *plot* function to create the graph, passing the *x* and *y* lists as arguments.
- In lines 9 and 10, we use the *xlabel* and *ylabel* functions to add labels to the X and Y axes, respectively.
- Finally, in line 11, we use the *show* function to display the graph.

Code and execute

1. import matplotlib.pyplot as plt
2.
3. # x represents the years
4. x = [2012, 2013, 2014, 2015, 2016, 2017]
5. # y represents the amount of money saved
6. y = [0, 50, 70, 70, 100, 246]
7.
8. plt.plot(x, y)
9. plt.xlabel("Year")
10. plt.ylabel("Savings (USD)")
11. plt.show()

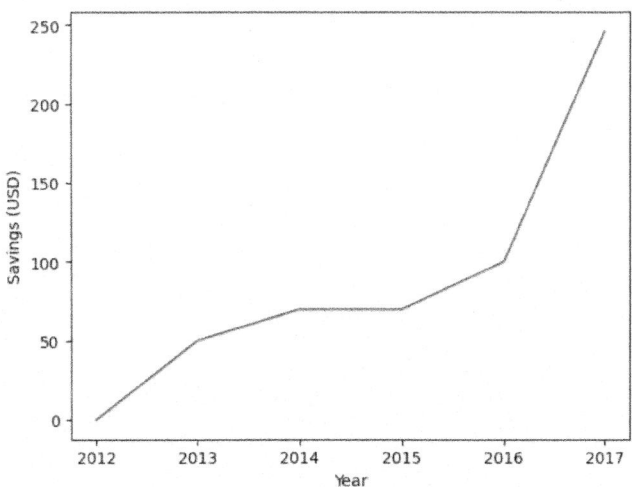

Figure 17-3. Execution of the previous code.

PyPlot bar function

The **bar** function in Python receives two arguments (two lists *x* and *y*) and draws a bar chart where *x* is a list with the bars' position on the X-axis, and *y* is a list with the height of the bars on the Y-axis. The following code shows how to use the *bar* function (see execution in Figure 17-4).
- In line 1, we import the *PyPlot* module with its respective alias.
- In line 4, we create a list *x* with the years.
- In line 6, we create a list *y* with the number of earthquakes per year.

- In line 8, we use the *bar* function to create the bar chart and pass the *x* and *y* lists as arguments.
- In lines 9 and 10, we define the labels for the X and Y axes, respectively.
- Finally, in line 11, we use the *show* function to display the bar chart.

Code and execute

1. import matplotlib.pyplot as plt
2.
3. # x represents the years
4. x = [2017, 2018, 2019, 2020, 2021]
5. # y represents the number of earthquakes
6. y = [1566, 1808, 1637, 1433, 2206]
7.
8. plt.bar(x, y)
9. plt.xlabel("Year")
10. plt.ylabel("Earthquakes")
11. plt.show()

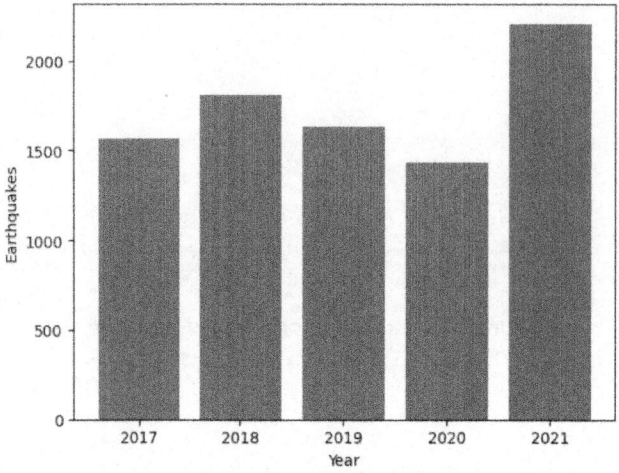

Figure 17-4. Execution of the previous code.

 **TIP:** Matplotlib offers a wide range of modules and functions for creating various types of graphs. If you want to explore more of these options, we suggest checking out this link: https://matplotlib.org/stable/gallery/index. You can find numerous examples of graphs you can create using this library.

17.5. Exercises

Theoretical exercises

E17.1. What Python reserved word is used when we want to import a library or module?

E17.2. What Python reserved word is used when we want to give an alias to an imported module or library?

E17.3. What is Matplotlib used for?

Practical exercises

E17.4. Create the necessary code to generate the following chart (see Figure 17-5).

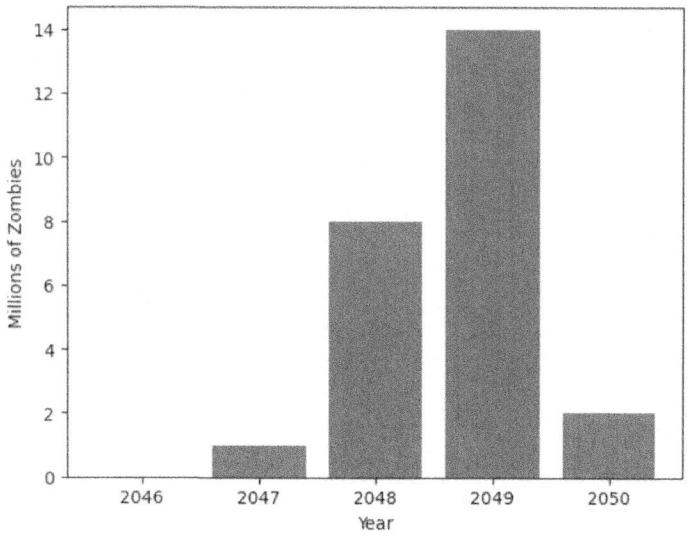

Figure 17-5. Chart year versus millions of Zombies.

Summary

In this chapter, we learned about how libraries work in Python. We learned that Python incorporates "The Python Standard Library" (which includes modules with useful functionalities that can be reused). We learned how to use the *math* and *random* modules from "The Python Standard Library". We learned about the Python Package Index (PyPI), where the Python community develops and shares projects or libraries to be used by anyone. And we learned how to use some functions from the *PyPlot* module of the Matplotlib library.

It was a long journey where we learned multiple elements of programming and Python. But before we finish, let's see in the next chapter how we can continue our learning journey in the world of Python and programming.

Chapter 18 – Continue your learning

We have learned a lot since we started this book. We took a practical approach to designing and implementing hundreds of small programs with Python, covering multiple concepts and elements. However, there are many elements that we did not develop in this book.

In this chapter, we will provide additional resources to continue your learning journey independently and practice your programming skills.

Next, we will cover the following sections:
1. Additional topics.
2. Platforms for practicing.
3. Final remarks and future books.

18.1. Additional topics

While this book has covered a lot of ground, other topics in Python were beyond its scope. Below, we have highlighted a few of these topics along with some useful links where you can learn more:
- **Tuples:** are a type of sequence data like lists, but once defined, a tuple cannot be modified (https://docs.python.org/3/tutorial/datastructures.html#tuples-and-sequences).
- **Sets:** are a type of sequence data like lists, but they cannot contain duplicated elements (https://docs.python.org/3/tutorial/datastructures.html#sets).
- **Exception handling:** allows you to modify how errors are presented to the end-user (https://docs.python.org/3/tutorial/errors.html#handling-exceptions).
- **Classes (Object-Oriented Programming):** allows you to define your own data types (https://docs.python.org/3/tutorial/classes.html).

18.2. Platforms for practicing

If you enjoyed the exercises in this book, you may find the following free resources to be useful supplements.

CodingBat

CodingBat is a website that provides free coding exercises and challenges for learning and practicing programming in Python and Java (https://codingbat.com/python). Users can register and track their progress on completed exercises or use the site without registering.

CodingBat exercises are programmed as functions. Figure 18-1 shows how to solve one of the exercises (https://codingbat.com/prob/p141905). Each exercise is verified by running test cases. On the right side of Figure 18-1, an example of the test cases for the exercise is presented, and if all the cases pass, the exercise is completed.

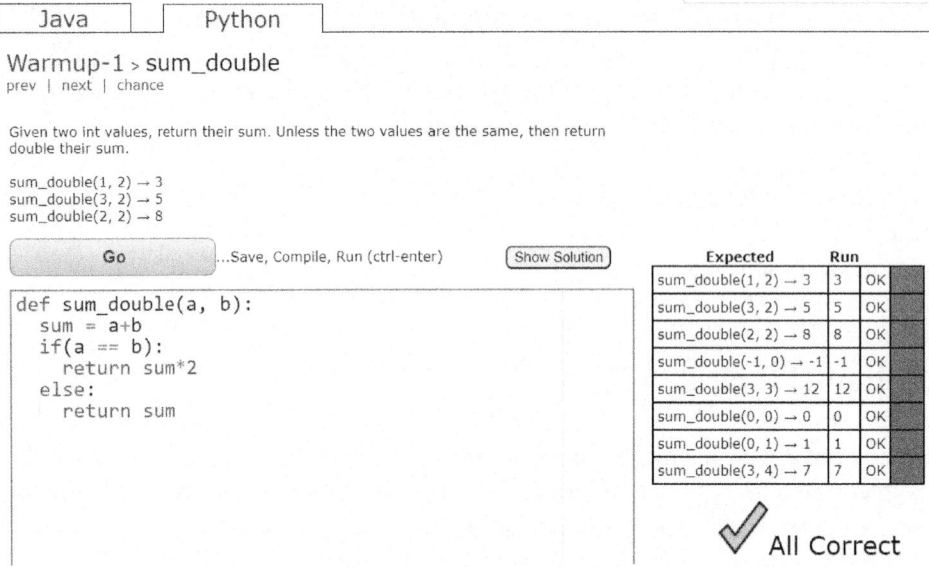

Figure 18-1. CodingBat exercise.

Codewars

Codewars is another platform like CodingBat that provides coding exercises and challenges in various programming languages (https://www.codewars.com/). This platform allows users to create their own exercises and share them with the community. While some exercises can be accessed and executed without registering, most require the user to be registered.

Figure 18-2 shows how to solve one of its exercises using functions (https://www.codewars.com/kata/56bc28ad5bdaeb48760009b0/train/python?collection=python-ders). Each exercise is tested using a set of test cases, and if all the test cases pass, the exercise is considered complete.

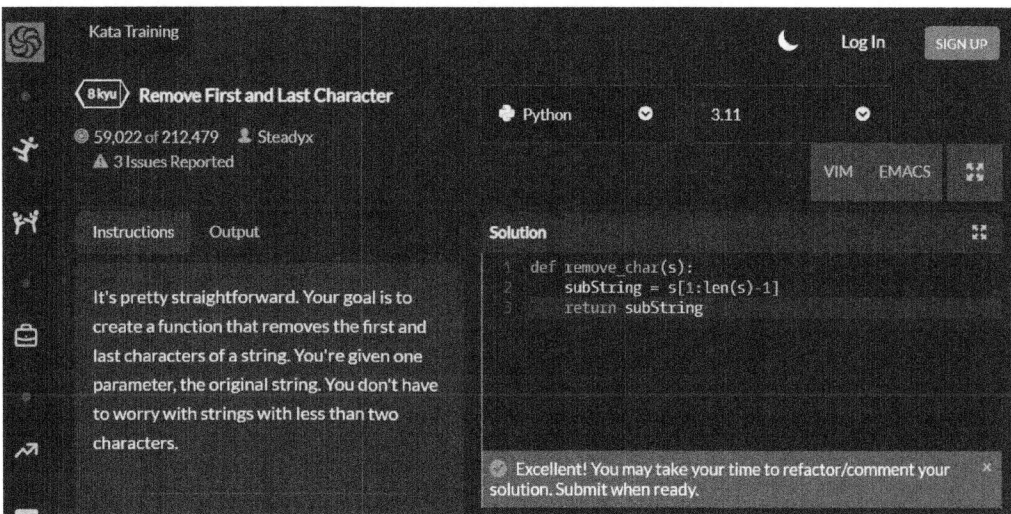

Figure 18-2. Codewars exercise.

Other platforms

In addition to the resources mentioned above, you can search on Google or use platforms such as freeCodeCamp, Codecademy, Code.org, or HackerRank.

18.3. Final remarks and future books

The authors of this book are also authors of other programming books. For example, Daniel has written six other books on web programming. One of these books is "Django 4 for the Impatient" (published in 2022), which teaches how to program web applications with Python. You can look at it at the following link: https://www.amazon.com/gp/product/B0B25BLDV4/.

Additionally, the authors of this book are constantly working on developing new books. If you want to stay informed, follow Daniel's Twitter account (**@danielgarax**).

Free extra chapters

To keep the book short, we developed an extra chapter (about tuples and sets) and another about a library project. If you would like to receive these chapters, please email us at practicalbooksco@gmail.com, and we will send them to you.

Comments

As book authors, we love to receive feedback from readers. If you would like, you can write to us at practicalbooksco@gmail.com and let us know what you liked and didn't like about this book. We take the opinions of our readers very seriously, and we will use them as a basis for developing future versions of this book or other books.

Book review

Finally, before ending this book, **we kindly ask you to leave an honest review on Amazon**. This is crucial for potential readers to know the unbiased opinion of people who have already read the book, and based on that information, they can decide to purchase the book. This process will only take a few minutes of your time, but it is very valuable to us.

And if Amazon does not allow you to submit a review, we greatly appreciate any mention on social media about the book.

"Hecho en Medellín" – "Made with Love"

Chapter 19 – Exercise solutions

In this chapter, we will present the solution to the theoretical and practical exercises proposed in some of the book's chapters. These solutions will not always coincide precisely with the answers you develop, as there are different ways to solve the same programming exercise.

The code developed for this chapter is located at https://github.com/PracticalBooks/Python-For-Beginners/tree/main/Chapter19.

19.1. Solutions to exercises in Chapter 05

E5.1. (i) *totalToPay* is *float*, (ii) *productName* is *str*, (iii) *satellites* is *int*, and (iv) *engines* is *str*.

E5.2. *print* is used to display information on the screen.

E5.3. Line 1, this is because the variable name "cat age" contains a space, which is not allowed in Python.

E5.4.

	Solution
1.	firstName = "Juan"
2.	lastName = "Pinzón"
3.	age = 19
4.	height = 168.2
5.	
6.	print(firstName)
7.	print(lastName)
8.	print(age)
9.	print(height)

19.2. Solutions to exercises in Chapter 06

E6.1. (i) *elonAge* is *int*, (ii) *bezosAge* is *str*, and (iii) *bezosAgeModified* is *int*.

E6.2. *input* allows the user to enter data into a program.

E6.3. *str()* function.

E6.4.

Solution

1. firstName = input("Enter your first name: ")
2. lastName = input("Enter your last name: ")
3. age = int(input("Enter your age: "))
4. height = float(input("Enter your height: "))
5.
6. print(firstName)
7. print(type(firstName))
8. print(lastName)
9. print(type(lastName))
10. print(age)
11. print(type(age))
12. print(height)
13. print(type(height))

E6.5.

Solution

1. firstName = input("Enter your first name: ")
2. lastName = input("Enter your last name: ")
3. print(lastName+" "+firstName)

E6.6.

Solution

1. estimatedYears = float(input("Enter the number of years: "))
2. realYears = estimatedYears/2
3. print("The asteroid will fall in: "+str(realYears)+" years")

19.3. Solutions to exercises in Chapter 07

E7.1. Lines 1, 2, and 4 are executed.

E7.2. The logical operator *and* is used to compare boolean variables or expressions. This operator evaluates to *True* only if both values or expressions are *True*.

E7.3.

Expression	Result
(load == 200) *and* (type != "Truck")	True
(load > 350) *or* (type == "Tractor")	True
(load <= 600) *and* (type != "Tractor")	False
not(type == "Truck")	True

E7.4.

Solution

1. distance = float(input("Enter the distance: "))
2. if(distance <= 4):
3.   print("I'm coming over")

E7.5.

Solution

1. jerseyNumber = int(input("Enter the jersey number: "))
2. if(jerseyNumber == 19):
3.   print("What are you looking at fool? Get back there")

E7.6.

Solution

1. magnitude = float(input("Enter the magnitude of the earthquake: "))
2. if(magnitude >= 5.2):
3.   print("Tsunami alert!!")

19.4. Solutions to exercises in Chapter 08

E8.1. Lines 1, 2, 4, 5, and 6 are executed.

E8.2. True.

E8.3. *Flappin flotsam, what's that - End of program*

E8.4.

Solution

```
1.  genre = input("Enter your favorite musical genre: ")
2.  if(genre == "Rock"):
3.    print("You have good taste")
4.  else:
5.    print("Disgusting")
```

E8.5.

Solution

```
1.  name1 = input("Enter the name of the first student: ")
2.  votes1 = int(input("Enter the vote count for first student: "))
3.  name2 = input("Enter the name of the second student: ")
4.  votes2 = int(input("Enter the vote count for second student: "))
5.
6.  if(votes1 > votes2):
7.    print(name1)
8.  elif(votes2 > votes1):
9.    print(name2)
10. else:
11.   print("Tie")
```

19.5. Solutions to exercises in Chapter 09

E9.1. Lines 1, 2, 3, 4, 2, 3, 4, 2, and 5 are executed.

E9.2. They are: (i) initialization of the control variable, (ii) test on the control variable, (iii) body of loop, and (iv) update on the control variable.

E9.3. *0 - 3 - 6*

E9.4.

Solution

```
1.   times = int(input("Enter a number: "))
2.   i = 1
3.   while(i <= times):
4.      print("****")
5.      i = i+1
```

E9.5.

Solution

```
1.   while(True):
2.      keyword = input("Enter the keyword: ")
3.      if(keyword == "Robert"):
4.         print("Correct keyword")
5.         break
6.      else:
7.         print("Incorrect keyword")
```

19.6. Solutions to exercises in Chapter 10

E10.1. *G - Gin - 3*

E10.2. The second argument that can be passed to the *find()* method is the start index, which specifies the starting index from where the search for the substring should begin.

E10.3. *y*

E10.4.

Solution

1. text = input("Enter a text: ")
2. firstChar = text[0]
3. lastChar = text[len(text)-1]
4. print(firstChar+lastChar)

E10.5.

Solution

1. text = input("Enter your text: ")
2. indexZ = text.find("z")
3. if(indexZ == -1):
4.   print("Text does not contain letter z")
5. else:
6.   print("Text contains letter z")

E10.6.

Solution

1. word = input("Enter your word: ")
2. i = 0
3. while(i < len(word)):
4.   if(word[i] != "a" and word[i] != "e" and word[i] != "i" and word[i] != "o" and word[i] != "u"):
5.   print(word[i])
6.   i = i+1

19.7. Solutions to exercises in Chapter 11

E11.1. *3 - Blue*

E11.2. *colors.pop(1)*

E11.3. Error. *IndexError: list index out of range.*

E11.4.

Solution

1. movies = []
2. i = 1
3. while(i <= 4):
4.   movie = input("Enter the name of your favorite movie: ")
5.   movies.append(movie)
6.   i = i+1
7.
8. print(movies)

E11.5.

Solution

1. secretMessage = ["Planet", "You", "Secret", "Are", "Zombie", "The", "Nuclear", "Alien"]
2.
3. i = 1
4. while(i < len(secretMessage)):
5.   print(secretMessage[i])
6.   i = i+2

19.8. Solutions to exercises in Chapter 12

E12.1. *Magician - float*

E12.2. We use a dictionary instead of a list when: (i) we want to store values of different types, (ii) we want to identify indexes with a key, or (iii) the order in which elements are stored is not important.

E12.3. (i) *dict*, (ii) *int*, (iii) *2*, and (iv) there is no key called *brand* (error).

E12.4.

Solution

```
1.   name = input("Enter the name of the pet: ")
2.   age = int(input("Enter the age of the pet: "))
3.   gender = input("Enter the gender of the pet: ")
4.
5.   pet = {
6.     "name":name,
7.     "age":age,
8.     "gender":gender
9.   }
10.
11.  print(pet)
```

E12.5.

Solution

```
1.   numTeams = int(input("Enter the number of teams: "))
2.   teams = []
3.
4.   i = 1
5.   while(i <= numTeams):
6.     name = input("Enter the name of the team: ")
7.     country = input("Enter the country of the team: ")
8.     team = {"name":name, "country":country}
9.     teams.append(team)
10.    i = i+1
11.
12.  print(teams)
```

19.9. Solutions to exercises in Chapter 13

E13.1. *Rocks - Rocks - Rocks - Rocks*

E13.2. start, stop, and step.

E13.3. Lines 1, 2, 3, 2, 3, 2, and 3 are executed.

E13.4.i.

Solution

1. for number in range(1,81):
2.   print(number)

E13.4.ii.

Solution

1. for number in range(1000,-1,-100):
2.   print(number)

E13.4.iii.

Solution

1. for number in range(2,67,2):
2.   print(number)

E13.5.

Solution

```
1.   names = []
2.   for number in range(4):
3.       name = input("Enter name: ")
4.       names.append(name)
5.
6.   for name in names:
7.       if(name[0] == "L"):
8.           print("Name discarded")
9.       else:
10.          print("Possible name")
```

19.10. Solutions to exercises in Chapter 14

E14.1. (i) *strangeOccurrence*, (ii) 1, (iii) no, (iv) 1, and (v) *I saw a UFO last night.*

E14.2. *return*

E14.3. Lines 5, 1, 2, 6, 1, 2, and 3 are executed.

E14.4.

Solution

```
1.   def printFirstName(names):
2.       print(names[0])
3.
4.   names = ["Zeus", "Poseidon", "Ares"]
5.   printFirstName(names)
```

E14.5. Given the length of this exercise, the solution can be found at: https://github.com/PracticalBooks/Python-For-Beginners/tree/main/Chapter19.

19.11. Solutions to exercises in Chapter 15

E15.1. A counter is used to keep track of the number of times an event has occurred, usually incrementing by 1 each time. Whereas an accumulator is used to accumulate values, and it doesn't always add the same amount.

E15.2. Lines 1, 3, 4, 6, 3, 4, and 5 are executed.

E15.3.

	Solution
1.	a1 = {"name":"2022 HX1", "distance":1547214}
2.	a2 = {"name":"2022 HA2", "distance":2870734}
3.	a3 = {"name":"101955 Bennu", "distance":20188350}
4.	asteroids = [a1, a2, a3]
5.	
6.	collisionCount = 0
7.	for asteroid in asteroids:
8.	if(asteroid["distance"] < 4660283):
9.	collisionCount = collisionCount+1
10.	
11.	print("Asteroids with high collision probability:"+str(collisionCount))

E15.4.

Solution

```
1.   a1 = {"name":"2022 HX1", "distance":1547214}
2.   a2 = {"name":"2022 HA2", "distance":2870734}
3.   a3 = {"name":"101955 Bennu", "distance":20188350}
4.   asteroids = [a1, a2, a3]
5.
6.   accumulator = 0
7.   for asteroid in asteroids:
8.       accumulator = accumulator+asteroid["distance"]
9.
10.  averageDistance = accumulator/len(asteroids)
11.  print("Average distance: "+str(averageDistance))
```

19.12. Solutions to exercises in Chapter 16

E16.1. The *read()* method is used for reading the contents of a file.

E16.2. The *readlines* method is used to read all the lines of a file and return them as a list of strings. Each element of the list corresponds to a line in the file.

E16.3. Given the length of this exercise, the solution can be found at: https://github.com/PracticalBooks/Python-For-Beginners/tree/main/Chapter19.

19.13. Solutions to exercises in Chapter 17

E17.1. *import*

E17.2. *as*

E17.3. Matplotlib is used to create static, animated, and interactive visualizations in Python.

E17.4.

	Solution
1.	import matplotlib.pyplot as plt
2.	
3.	x = [2046, 2047, 2048, 2049, 2050]
4.	y = [0, 1, 8, 14, 2]
5.	
6.	plt.bar(x, y)
7.	plt.xlabel("Year")
8.	plt.ylabel("Millions of Zombies")
9.	plt.show()

Printed in Great Britain
by Amazon